Self-Sovereign Identity: Privacy, Key Management, and Decentralized Access Control

Faizan

Table of Contents

List of Tables

Chapter 1

Introduction

Self-Sovereign Identity (SSI) is a transformative paradigm in digital identity management that shifts authority from centralized entities to individuals. It enables users to control the issuance, storage, and disclosure of their identity credentials without depending on intermediaries. This dissertation presents novel technical contributions that extend the capabilities of SSI systems, address critical challenges in privacy and usability, and demonstrate their applicability in real-world domains such as regulatory compliance and digital asset authentication.

Digital identity refers to the set of electronically captured attributes, credentials, and identifiers that describe an entity and enable its authentication in digital systems [1]. These may include personal information, biometric data, cryptographic keys, and contextual metadata. Digital identities serve as proxies for real-world entities and are used across domains such as finance, healthcare, and e-government services.

There are three dominant models for managing digital identities today [2, 3]:

- **Siloed Identity**: Each organization issues and controls its own credentials for users, resulting in isolated identity repositories with no interoperability across systems.
- **Federated Identity**: A centralized identity provider enables users to authenticate across multiple platforms. While this improves convenience, it concentrates control and surveillance in the hands of a few entities.
- **User-Centric Identity**: Users are granted partial control over their identity credentials, typically through vendor-managed wallets or identity hubs, but the underlying

architecture still relies on centralized verification systems.

Self-Sovereign Identity represents a fourth modelone that grants individuals full ownership of their identity data through decentralized identifiers (DIDs), verifiable credentials (VCs), and cryptographic proofs [4, 5]. SSI systems reduce reliance on trusted third parties, support selective disclosure, and enable secure, privacy-preserving interactions across domains.

While SSI is conceptually promising, its practical deployment introduces new challenges. For example how to recover lost keys without introducing centralized risks, or how to enforce user-defined access policies, and how to apply SSI in domains such as financial compliance or Web3 authentication. This dissertation addresses these issues by introducing original frameworks, protocols, and algorithms that enhance the technical maturity and usability of SSI.

1.1 Motivations

Legacy identity systems are no longer sufficient for modern digital ecosystems. Centralized identity providers act as single points of failureprone to data breaches, surveillance, and loss of user control. As data privacy concerns grow, these systems struggle to meet the demands of transparency, consent, and minimal disclosure.

Users often lack visibility into how their data is stored or shared. In jurisdictions with inadequate privacy protections, identity data can be accessed by governments or private actors without the user's knowledge. The invalidation of the EU–U.S. Privacy Shield by the Court of Justice of the European Union in the *Schrems II* case [6] illustrates the geopolitical implications of centralized data control.

A further limitation of the current identity ecosystem is exclusion. More than one billion people worldwide lack access to recognized digital identities [7], which hinders access to essential services including healthcare, banking, and social programs [8]. Without an inclusive, user-controlled identity framework, this gap will continue to grow.

Authentication mechanisms also remain problematic. Password-based systems are not only inconvenient, but also insecurevulnerable to phishing, credential stuffing, and social engineering. Users often reuse weak credentials, leading to frequent compromises and account takeovers.

Meanwhile, the regulatory landscape is evolving. Laws such as the GDPR have placed new obligations on organizations to limit data collection and enable user rights such as data portability and consent management. However, compliance is difficult to achieve in traditional systems that require central data aggregation.

Recent advances in verifiable credentials, decentralized identity protocols, and privacy-preserving cryptography create the opportunity for a paradigm shift. SSI offers a path toward secure, privacy-aware, and user-centric identity ecosystems.

The following points summarize how SSI mitigates the limitations of traditional digital identity systems:

- **Single Point of Failure → Decentralization:** SSI eliminates reliance on centralized identity providers by using decentralized identifiers and blockchain-based registries. Users maintain control of their credentials, reducing systemic vulnerability to data breaches and provider outages.

- **Lack of Transparency → User-Centric Data Control:** Users explicitly manage when, how, and with whom their credentials are shared. Verifiable credentials support selective disclosure, enabling minimal data sharing tailored to specific interactions.

- **Surveillance Risks → Privacy by Design:** SSI systems use zero-knowledge proofs and privacy-preserving cryptography to validate claims without revealing unnecessary personal information. Credentials are stored locally or in user-controlled agents, avoiding centralized databases that can be surveilled.

- **Exclusion → Global Accessibility and Inclusivity:** SSI frameworks are device-agnostic and internet-accessible, enabling issuance and verification of credentials without national ID systems. SSI can also support informal or community-based credentials, expanding identity inclusion in underserved populations.

- **Insecure Authentication → Cryptographic Security:** SSI replaces password-based authentication with cryptographic key pairs and verifiable presentations. Phishing and credential reuse risks are significantly reduced as authentication is bound to the user's private keys.

- **Regulatory Compliance Challenges → Data Minimization and Consent:** SSI aligns with General Data Protection Regulation (GDPR) and similar laws by enabling data portability, informed consent, and user revocation capabilities. It eliminates the need for data replication across systems, reducing compliance risk and improving auditability.

Despite significant progress in SSI research, existing work remains fragmented across architectural design, domain-specific applications, privacy engineering, and governance. Prior studies have largely focused on isolated aspects of SSI, leaving a gap in unified and deployable system design. Foundational research establishes the conceptual basis of SSI, emphasizing decentralization and user control, but often lacks practical considerations for scalability and system integration. Architectural frameworks and protocol-level solutions provide important insights; however, they introduce trade-offs between security, usability, and decentralization without fully addressing challenges such as key management and interoperability. Domain-specific implementations in areas such as healthcare, finance, and education demonstrate the feasibility of SSI; however, these solutions are typically tailored to narrow use cases and do not generalize well across domains. Advances in privacy-preserving technologies, including attribute-based encryption, zero-knowledge proofs, and secure multi-party computation, enhance confidentiality and selective disclosure. Nevertheless, these techniques are commonly applied as standalone components and are not integrated into a cohesive and practically deployable framework for enforcing access control and data governance. Similarly, existing approaches to access control in SSI lack strong cryptographic binding between data and policy, relying instead on external enforcement mechanisms. This creates a gap between policy definition and enforcement, increasing the risk of misuse after data disclosure. Overall, current research advances individual components of SSI or proposes stand-alone solutions, but does not deliver an integrated architecture that combines secure key management, cryptographically enforced access control, privacy-preserving data sharing, and practical deployability.

These observations can be distilled into a set of concrete technical and architectural challenges:

C1 **Key Recovery:** SSI relies on users to manage their own cryptographic keys. If a private key is lost or compromised, there is no built-in, standardized way to recover it without reintroducing centralized control or weakening security.

C2 **Access Control:** While SSI enables credential-based verification, there is no native mechanism for users to define and enforce fine-grained access policies over their personal data across different platforms and verifiers.

C3 **Fraud and Authenticity in Digital Assets:** In applications like Web3 or Non-Fungible Tokens authentication, current SSI approaches do not fully address the provenance and identity-binding requirements needed to prevent forgery and digital asset fraud.

C4 **Usability and Adoption:** Managing identifiers such as Decentralized Identifiers, credentials, and digital wallets can be complex for non-technical users. Lack of intuitive interfaces, interoperability between wallet providers, and clear onboarding processes limits mass adoption.

C5 **Interoperability and Standards Fragmentation:** Despite efforts from groups like W3C and DIF, the ecosystem still suffers from partial implementations, vendor-specific formats, and incompatibility between SSI networks and protocols.

C6 **Regulatory Integration:** While SSI aligns with privacy laws like the GDPR, regulators and institutions often lack the frameworks or technical expertise to integrate decentralized identity into existing compliance workflows.

C7 **Credential Verification at Scale:** Ensuring real-time, trustworthy verification of credentials across domains (e.g., finance, healthcare, web3) poses scalability and latency challenges.

These challenges reveal several fundamental gaps in the current SSI ecosystem. Addressing these gaps requires advances in key management, data governance, and application-layer integration. The research presented in this dissertation is guided by the following research questions.

- **Research Question 1:** How can users securely manage their cryptographic keys in a way that balances convenience, security, and privacy?
- **Research Question 2:** How can users enforce granular access control policies on their personal data while ensuring interoperability and usability?
- **Research Question 3:** How can SSI architectures support real-world identity applications such as regulatory compliance and authenticated digital assets?

The chapters that follow present solutions to these research questions through a sequence of architectural and application-level contributions that collectively strengthen the SSI ecosystem.

1.2 Contributions

The contributions of this dissertation are structured as a layered enhancement of the self-sovereign identity ecosystem. First, we address foundational infrastructure challenges by proposing a decentralized key recovery model for SSI wallets. Second, we extend the data governance capabilities of SSI by introducing a privacy-preserving access control framework that enables users to enforce fine-grained policies on their personal data. Building on these foundational capabilities, we demonstrate how SSI can be applied to real-world domains through two application scenarios: regulatory identity verification and authenticated digital assets. Together, these contributions form a cohesive architecture that advances SSI from conceptual identity management toward deployable privacy-preserving digital infrastructure.

Formally, this dissertation introduces new frameworks and system designs that advance the state of the art in self-sovereign identity. This dissertation argues that by addressing key infrastructure challenges such as secure key recovery and user-controlled data access policies, self-sovereign identity can evolve from a conceptual identity paradigm into a deployable architecture capable of supporting real-world digital identity applications.

Each contribution of this dissertation addresses a core limitation in SSI design or deployment:

- **Key Recovery Model:** We propose a novel approach to key recovery for SSI users, ensuring secure and efficient retrieval of identity credentials in the event of key loss or compromise. **This work addresses RQ1 and challenges C1 and C4.**
- **Access Management Framework:** We develop an access control enforcement mechanism that allows users to enforce data sharing policies while preserving privacy. **This work addresses RQ2 and challenges C2 and C5.**
- **KYC Enhancement via SSI:** We propose an SSI-based model to streamline Know

Your Customer (KYC) processes, reduce repeated identity verification while improving regulatory compliance and minimizing data exposure risks. **This work corresponds to RQ3 and challenges C4, C6 and C7.**

- **SSI-Backed Non-Fungible Tokens (NFTs):** We propose a novel approach for an identity-bound NFT issuance framework that combines verifiable credentials with blockchain assets to prevent forgery and strengthen provenance. **This work corresponds to RQ3 and challenge C3.**

These contributions are supported by formal models, implementations, and evaluations of usability and performance. Collectively, they demonstrate the technical maturity and deployability of SSI in high-assurance environments.

1.3 Organization

This dissertation is structured as follows:

- **Chapter 1: Introduction** Defines the scope of the dissertation, introduces key concepts, and outlines the motivation, contributions, and research questions.
- **Chapter 2: Identity Management** Surveys traditional and emerging identity models, including a detailed examination of the architectural foundations of self-sovereign identity.
- **Chapter 3: Key Recovery in SSI** Proposes a secure and user-centric key recovery model for decentralized identity systems.
- **Chapter 4: Access Policy Enforcement** Develops a novel mechanism for enforcing privacy-preserving data sharing policies using SSI technologies.
- **Chapter 5: SSI in KYC Compliance** Demonstrates how SSI can be leveraged to improve regulatory compliance in Know Your Customer processes.

- **Chapter 6: SSI in NFT Authentication** Explores how SSI can strengthen NFT authentication and prevent forgery through identity-bound asset issuance.
- **Chapter 7: Conclusion and Future Directions** Summarizes findings, evaluates the research questions, and identifies future work in the field of decentralized identity.

The contributions of this dissertation can be understood as a layered architecture that strengthens the SSI ecosystem from foundational infrastructure to application deployment. Figure 1.1 illustrates this layered architecture.

This organization reflects a progression from foundational concepts to applied innovations. The goal is to demonstrate that SSI can address pressing challenges in digital identity management and serve as a foundational layer for future privacy-respecting digital ecosystems. While existing research has explored the theoretical foundations of self-sovereign identity [2, 9, 10], practical deployment requires addressing multiple interdependent challenges across infrastructure, data governance, and application integration. This dissertation contributes to each of these layers, presenting a coherent set of innovations that collectively strengthen the usability, security, and applicability of SSI systems.

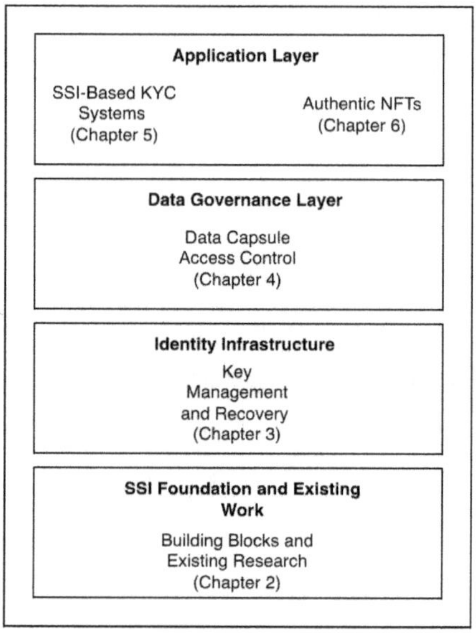

Figure 1.1: Layered Architecture of Contributions

Chapter 2

Identity Management

This chapter provides a comprehensive overview of identity, digital identity, and Identity and Access Management (IAM). We begin by introducing the fundamental concept of identity and its role in both physical and digital interactions, followed by a discussion of digital identity and the challenges associated with representing and managing identities in online environments. Figure 2.1 illustrates the conceptual progression of identity technologies discussed throughout this chapter.

We then examine how digital identities are managed through Identity and Access Management systems and trace the evolution of identity management models, from isolated and centralized architectures to federated and user-centric approaches. This progression sets the stage for the emergence of Self-Sovereign Identity, a decentralized paradigm that enables individuals to control their personal data while enhancing security and privacy. In this research, we argue that SSI represents not merely an incremental improvement over previous models but a fundamental shift in the architecture of digital identity.

Building on this foundation, the chapter introduces the core technologies and architectural components that support SSI, including decentralized identifiers, verifiable credentials, authentication mechanisms, trust frameworks, and privacy-preserving cryptographic protocols. We further review major platforms, technical standards, and regulatory frameworks that shape the modern digital identity ecosystem.

By establishing this technical and conceptual foundation, the chapter motivates the novel mechanisms and architectural enhancements proposed in the subsequent chapters.

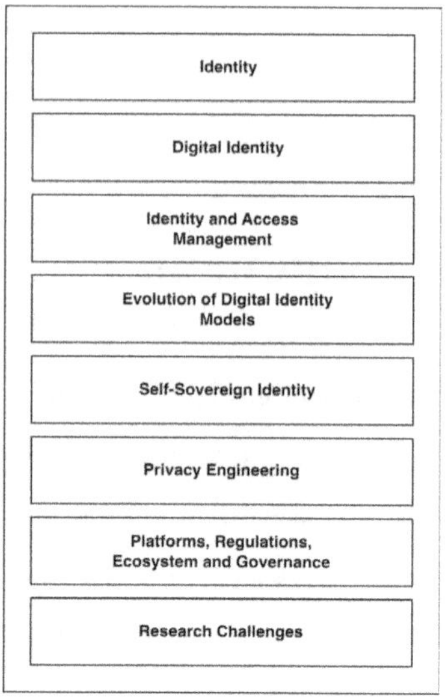

Figure 2.1: Conceptual structure of identity technologies leading to Self-Sovereign Identity.

2.1 Identity

As an important concept in many fields of study including psychology and sociology, the concept of identity has a long intellectual history [11]. The exact definition of identity is highly context specific [12]. The American Heritage Dictionary defines identity as 'The set of characteristics by which a person or thing is definitively recognizable or known', and 'The fact or condition of being the same as something else'. [13].

The word identity originated from the Middle French "identit", which is derived from Late Latin "identitat-, identitas", from Latin "identidem", which is a contraction of "idem et idem" , meaning "same and same" [14].

Although the term "identity" is widely used across disciplines and in everyday discourse, it is rather difficult to provide an adequate and concise explanation to encompass its every meaning [15].

The French philosopher Paul Ricoeur defines identity as two-fold. The first is known as *Idem* which means sameness in Latin [16], and the second aspect is defined as *Ipse* meaning selfhood in Latin [16]. The sameness feature represents the characteristics that remain unchanged, and the selfhood aspect represents the features that are unique. From that definition, identity can be defined as the representation of an *entity* through features that make the entity unique and/or persist through time, in a given context. The term *entity* is defined as a logical or physical object with a separate distinctive existence either in a logical or physical sense [17].

In the field of psychology, the term is generally referred to all the psychological traits of a person, including beliefs, personality and other attributes [18]. While in sociology, the concept of identity includes the history, culture, religion and traditions associated to the person [19].

The modern definition of identity as we know it was first used in 1950 by Erik Erikson, and has been used in various context and purposes [20].

U. Glsser et al. define identity as a logical representation of a physical presence of a person or thing [21].Wang and De Filippi define identity as all attributes of a person that uniquely defines the person over the course of a lifetime, providing sameness and continuity despite varying aspects and conditions [10].

Finally, In the book "Identity is the New Money" [22], David Birch projected the next evolution of identity to be defined by our social graphs, which take the model back to a digitized version of the pre-industrial approach. The social graph is a digital representation of our truthful relationships.

2.2 Digital Identity

A digital identity is the unique representation of an entity within a particular digital context.

The National Institute of Standards and Technology (NIST) [23] defines digital identity as "the unique representation of a subject engaged in an online transaction. A digital identity is always unique in the context of a digital service, but does not necessarily need to uniquely identify the subject in all contexts. In other words, accessing a digital service may not mean that the subjects real-life identity is known.". The International Telecommunication Union (ITU) [24] defines digital identity as 'A digital representation of the information known about a specific individual, group or organization'

2.2.1 The Laws of Identity

Kim Cameron defines digital identity as "a set of claims made by one digital subject about itself or another digital subject" [1]. He also introduces the *Seven Laws of Identity*. These laws are as follows:

1. Users should be in control of how their identity information is shared.
2. The amount of information disclosed should only be the minimum necessary amount required, and data should not be kept longer than needed by the other entities.
3. The user should be well informed about which entities manage their identity information.
4. The user's information should not be created or exposed in such a way to allow data correlation, pattern recognition, or entity identification by unauthorized entities.
5. Interoperability and seamless integration among various entities supported by different architecture should be possible.
6. Should empower reliable and secure integration between human users and machines.
7. Consistent user experience across multiple contexts and technologies

A *partial identity* or *persona* is a subset of identity attributes associated with an entity in a particular context [25]. For every entity there can be multiple partial identities. Digital identities are not necessarily the same as real-world identities since the digital identities represented online may differ from the characteristics of the identities in the physical world.

Indeed, there are various definitions of digital identity. These definitions are mostly inconsistent and semantics based. A definition founded on mathematical properties would help in providing a uniform definition of digital identity and reduce confusion [26].

Proposed by S. Ferdous, a *domain* can be defined as the namespace in which an entity is represented and uniquely identified. Assuming D denotes the set of domains and $d \in D$ defines the domain of a single organization whereas U_D stands for the set of users in that domain. It's possible to define A_d as the set of attributes and AV_d as the set of values for those attributes within d. We can then describe the attributes for a user in a particular domain d as:

$$atEntToVal_d : A_d \times U_d \rightarrow AV_d$$

The above function returns the corresponding value of the attributes in domain d. The function is a partial function as not every entity has a value for every attribute.

An *identifier* is a unique value used to distinguish an entity in a given a domain [26]. The identifier $i \in A_d$ in domain d is defined as an attribute that always exist and is unique within the context. These conditions can be defined as:

a) $atEntToVal_d(i, u)$ is defined for all $u \in U_d$

b) $\forall u_1, u_2 \in U_d,\ u_1 \neq u_2 \Rightarrow atEntToVal_d(i, u_1) \neq atEntToVal_d(i, u_2)$

The partial identity of a user u, for a domain d can then be described as:

$$parIdent_d^u = \{(a, v) | a \in A_d, atEntToVal_d(a, u) = v\}$$

which can be rewritten as

$$parIdent_d^u = \{(i_d, v_{i_d}), (a_1, v_1), (a_2, v_2), (a_3, v_3), .., (a_{n-1}, v_{n-1})\}$$

where the i_d and v_{i_d} represent the identifier and its corresponding value in domain d.

Finally, the complete identity of an entity is defined as the union of all their partial identities in all domains. This can be defined as:

$$ident^u = \bigcup\{(d, parIdent_d^u) | d \in D \text{ and } u \in U_d\}$$

By formalizing the concepts related to digital identity using mathematical properties, it is possible to describe and conceptualize the notions in a more formal and rigorous method and to capture the associated fundamental properties [9].

Having defined identity and digital identity, it is necessary to examine how these identities are managed in operational systems. Identity and Access Management frameworks provide the policies, mechanisms, and technologies used to manage identities and control access to digital resources.

2.3 Digital Identity Management

While digital identity describes how individuals and entities are represented in digital environments, practical systems must also manage how these identities are created, authenticated, and authorized across services.

This function is performed by Identity and Access Management (IAM) systems. IAM frameworks define the policies, technologies, and operational processes used to manage digital identities and control access to resources. The following section introduces the core components and operations of IAM systems.

An identity and access management system is a collection of tools, processes and policies used to manage individual identities, their authentication, authorization, roles and privileges, within an organization or across boundaries [27],[17]. An IAM system facilitates the administration of identities belonging to entities of an organization or a network. It keeps track of the roles and privileges associated with individual identities, and provides the decision makers with means of control access to sensitive resources. Being an $8 bil-

Figure 2.2: "On the internet, nobody knows you're a dog" - The New Yorker magazine (1993)

lion industry in 2016, a $20 Billion in 2020 [28] and a $42.12 Billion industry in 2024 [29], the goal of an IAM system is to increase security and productivity and decrease downtime, cost, and repetitive tasks such as user creation and deletion.

As the famous New Yorker cartoon "on the internet, nobody knows you're a dog" as shown in 2.2 says [30], there is a lack of adequate identity component on the Internet which has led to significant missed opportunities, as having accurate and trustworthy identity of users is crucial to the growth of the digital economy.

To accurately define identity and access management, it is important to begin by describing a number of fundamental terminologies.

Subjects are entities, such as people or things that are under consideration [1]. A subject is able to access an *object*. An object is a passive entity that is being accessed by a subject. An example of an object is a particular online service such as a bank account.

In identity systems, a subject may be a human user, organization, device, or application that interacts with a system and requests access to resources. In this dissertation, the term user refers specifically to a human subject interacting with the system and more generally, the term entity is used to denote any identifiable participant within the identity ecosystem, including individuals, organizations, devices, or software agents. While a subject typically represents the active role of an entity within a security transaction, the concept of an entity is broader and refers to any object that can possess identity attributes or be represented within an identity management framework.

As stated, *Identifiers* are labels given to subjects. Identifiers are used to keep track of the information known about the subjects in a specific context. Examples of identifiers include social insurance numbers in Canada, social security numbers in the United States, and driver's license numbers. An entity may have multiple identifiers.

Attributes describe the characteristic of an entity. An attribute is a distinct and measurable name-value property belonging to an entity in a given context. The value of an attribute may be used to identify the entity. Albeit the identification may not be unique to the entity [26].

Attributes can be issued by the entity itself or by another entity issuing them. Political affiliations, religious opinions, and gender are attributes that can typically be defined by the entity itself. There are also attributes assigned by one user to another. Attributes that can assist in the revealing or tracing of an individual's identity are known as Personal Identifiable Information (PII) [31].

A statement about an entity is known as a *claim*. Kim Cameron defines claim as "an assertion of the truth of something, typically one which is disputed or in doubt" [1]. A *credential* is a set of one or more claims made by the same entity. A *verifiable credential* is a set of tamper-evident claims and metadata that cryptographically prove who issued it [32].

Financial institutes, government agencies, and telecommunication companies are among potential trusted parties able to issue claims. The term *trust* is defined as "the firm belief in the truth or ability of someone or something to perform a task in a reliable matter, in a specific context" [33].

The main actors participating in IAM operations are shown in Figure 2.3. The *user* is a natural person with at least one digital identity that wishes to conduct a transaction. [34]. An *Identity Provider* (IdP) is a special type of service provider that manages identity

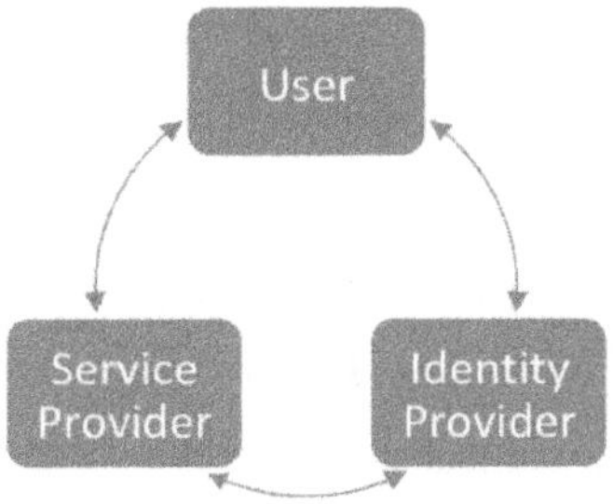

Figure 2.3: Identity Management Actors

Figure 2.4: Identity Management Operations

information. It is responsible for the creation, maintenance, and deletion of identity information belonging to the users. An IdP provides user authentication on behalf of the service providers [34]. A *Relying Party* (RP) or *Service Provider* (SP) is an entity that decides to provide its services, based on the information provided by other parties such as an identity provider and the user itself [34].

2.3.1 Operations of Identity and Access Management

Identity and access management systems provide a number of fundamental operations. As shown in Figure 2.4 they include Identification, Verification, Authentication, and Authorization.

Identification is generally the initial step towards recognizing the identity of subject. Identification occurs when a subject such as a user or a machine claims an identity. This process is typically accomplished by presenting a username, a unique ID, or anything that can uniquely identify the subject.

Relevant to identification, the *Zooko's triangle* published in an article by Bryze Wilcon-

OHearn in 2001 describes the three design decisions of an identification system to generate user identifiers. These designs decisions are *secure*, *decentralized*, and *human-meaningful*, out of which only two are likely achievable at the same time [35].

The next step after identification is sometimes the *identity verification* operation. Also known as identity proofing, and as relatively newer process, verification is the process by which specific identity attributes are truthfully associated with the entity they represent.

The *Authentication* operation involved verifying the identity of an entity such as user, process, or device, often as a prerequisite to allowing access to a systems resources [23]. This operation is typically achieved by an entity presenting a token, password, or other forms of information such as biometrics prior to accessing a protected resource.

Multi-Factor Authentication (MFA) is an authentication model that relies on more than one distinct authentication factor for a successful authentication. Authentication factors can be distinguished into four categories: First factor authentication corresponds to something the entity knows. A common instance of knowledge factor is a password, or a pin number known only by the entity and the recipient. Second factor authentication is attributed to something the entity possesses. Proving the possession of a mobile phone or a hard token are examples of this form of authentication. Third factor authentication represents what the entity is; this is typically achieved through biometrics such as fingerprint scan or facial recognition. Biometric authentication has been researched extensively in the recent years with many standards developed. For example the FIDO alliance [36] and The IEEE 2410 Biometric Open Protocol Standard (BOPS) [37] provide standards for secure, interoperable and seamless biometric based authentication.

Lastly, the fourth factor authentication is commonly attributed to authentication based on contextual information such as time, location, behavioral patterns, and the entity's social reputation.

Continuous authentication provides unobtrusive and continuous user authentication, behind the scene, and without inconveniencing the users. The user may have zero to limited knowledge of the authentication process happening, while they interact with the service provider. Continuous authentication can be a supplement to the more traditional authentication forms to better guarantee the established identity of the user who has been authenticated at the beginning of their session. Moreover, the continuous authentication process provides a level of identity assurance that may not be present with traditional authentication systems that take place only during the initial user interaction. Continuous authentication actively monitors the behavior of the user to ensure the behavioral patterns match those of the expected and previously calculated authorized user. If there is any deviation, a red flag may be raised by the service, which may prompt the user to re-authenticate with their credentials.

Authorization is the process of granting access rights to an entity such a user or a program. The authorization process determines what the entity can do against a target resource.

A combination of identification, authentication, authorization, and audit processes working in tandem to ensure only authorized entities are allowed to access the resources is called *access control* [38]. There are many common access control models. They include Discretionary Access control (DAC), Mandatory Access Control (MAC), Identity-based access control (IBAC), Label-based access control (LBAC), Policy-based access control (PBAC), Role-based access control (RBAC), Capability-based access control (CBAC) [39], and finally, Attribute-based access control (ABAC). Midhun et al. elaborates on existing access control models suitable for web applications [40].

2.3.2 Evolution of Identity Management Models

To address the evolving identity management requirements and provide users authenticated access to online service, various identity management models have been designed [41],[42]. Figure 2.5 illustrates this progression, moving from isolated to centralized, federated, and ultimately user-centric models. As Figure 2.5 shows we distinguish between five types of IAM architectures: isolated, central, federated, user-centric, and self-sovereign.

Figure 2.5: Evolution of four identity management models

2.3.3 Isolated Model

The *isolated identity model* or siloed identity model is one of the more preliminary forms of IAM in which the service provider is responsible for all identity management operations of its users. The major drawbacks of this approach is the large number of credentials that must be maintained by each user, and the risks associated with the storage of large amount of user data by every service provider. [41].

2.3.4 Centralized Model

Related to the above model, is the *centralized identity model* in which the identity provider and the service providers are decoupled and the identity provider acts as a central authority that manages identity data and authentication for multiple services. As depicted in Figure 2.6 every user interaction with the service providers must be authenticated through the central identity provider [41],[42]. It's important to note that centralized model does not indicate a centralized IT infrastructure, but rather the centralized management of identity data, including the user's unique identifier, and all identity management operations such as issuance, authentication, and handling of digital identity life cycle. The centralized model is susceptible to various security attacks. For example, the disclosure of a user's credential is sufficient for giving access to all other services associated with that user. The centralized approach of this model is not an efficient and ideal approach for Internet users or users of significantly large organizations. Examples of this model are Kerberos[43] and public key infrastructure (PKI) [44] based architecture such as one-tier hierarchy and other hierarchy options that rely on a single root central authority (CA) to issue, maintain and

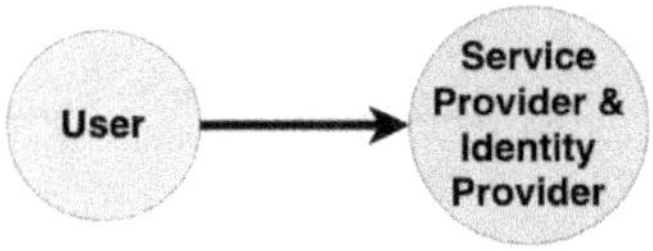

Figure 2.6: Centralized Identity Model

revoke digital certificates [45]. A CA can misuse certificates, issue invalid certificates [46], or become the victim of a security breach leading to a wide-ranging ramification including fraudulent issuance of certificates, man in the middle (MITM) and impersonation attacks [47],[48],[49]. When a CA is identified as compromised, all digital certificates issues by that CA are considered invalid. As a result, a rapid software update must be rolled out to all clients relying on that CA as a root of trust to remove the affected root certificates. The PKI and decentralized PKI models will be explained in detail in Section 4.4.

2.3.5 Federated Model

In the *federated model*, a set of service providers and identity providers form a *trusted* federation. As shown in Figure 2.7 This allows the user to have the option of authenticating through one of the federated identity providers to access any of the participating service providers.

The federated identity model allows a user to use a single set of credentials to authenticate with the identity provider, to seamlessly access any of the federated service providers. This is achieved by the identity provider providing an authentication token to the service provider. This model is the enabler of *Single-Sign On* [50].

Protocols such as Security Assertion Markup Language (SAML) [51] are leveraged to develop Federated identity systems.

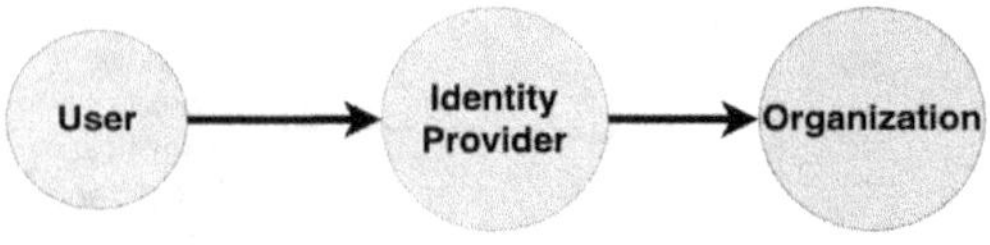

Figure 2.7: Federated Identity Model

2.3.6 User-Centric Model

Often expressed as a little discussed yet significant iteration in IAM models, the *user-centric identity model* allows users to have some liberty on selecting their preferred identity provider and the identity attribute they like to share, along with the conditions under which those attributes should be shared [41]. In this model, the service providers and the identity providers may not always have a pre-existing trust relationship. Examples of this model are the use of Facebook and Google login feature to access other online services. Protocols such as OAuth [52] and OpenID Connect [53] are the dominant technologies in this model. Hasnae L'Amrani et al. [54] provide an in-depth evaluation of aforementioned identity models.

2.3.7 OAuth

The OAuth 1.0 protocol was proposed in April 2010 by Eran Hammer-Lahav. The second version, OAuth 2.0, was introduced in 2012 by Dick Hardt [55]. The protocol provides a standardized method for accessing server resources on behalf of a resource owner and enables access without sharing credentials.

2.3.8 OpenID

The OpenID protocol, developed in 2005 by Brad Fitzpatrick, is an open standard for decentralized authentication. It allows users to create an account with an OpenID Provider (OP) and use this account to authenticate with third-party services, known as Relying Parties (RP), without needing to create new credentials for each service.

This approach is beneficial when the OpenID Provider is a trustworthy and long-lasting entity. However, users have no guarantee that the provider will remain operational or maintain its integrity over time, posing potential risks.

OpenID is distinct from the OAuth protocol. While OpenID is specifically designed for identity authentication, enabling users to verify who they are, OAuth is strictly focused on authorization, managing access control to resources without necessarily proving a user's identity.

2.3.9 SAML

The Security Assertion Markup Language (SAML) is an XML-based framework for exchanging authentication and authorization data between security domains. It enables secure, standardized identity federation, allowing users to authenticate once and gain access to multiple systems without needing to re-enter credentials.

SAML was primarily developed to facilitate web browser-based single sign-on (SSO), enabling seamless authentication across different web applications and services. However, its modular and extensible design allows it to be adapted for other use cases, including cloud identity management, enterprise authentication, and federated identity systems.

By leveraging SAML, organizations can enhance security, improve user experience, and reduce password-related risks while maintaining centralized control over identity management.

2.3.10 Web of Trust

The Web of Trust is a decentralized public-key authentication system originally built on Pretty Good Privacy (PGP). It was developed in the early 1990s by Philip R. Zimmermann as a model for establishing trust in digital communications without relying on centralized authorities.

Unlike traditional Public Key Infrastructure (PKI), where a centralized Certificate Authority (CA) vouches for identities, the Web of Trust allows individuals to act as both end-users and certification authorities. Users can authenticate and verify each other's public keys by digitally signing them, forming a distributed trust network. This approach enables users to build confidence in the authenticity of a public key based on endorsements from multiple trusted parties [56].

By leveraging this trust model, users can create their own Web of Trust, where confidence in an identity grows through a network of interlinked signatures. While this system provides flexibility and decentralization, it also has limitations, such as scalability challenges and the subjectivity of trust relationships, making it less suited for large-scale enterprise environments compared to hierarchical PKI models.

The most suitable model and configuration of an identity management system adopted by an organization depend on various cultural, historical, jurisdictional, and technical factors. Each type of identity management model is designed to meet specific requirements [41].

2.4 Self-Sovereign Identity

The progression from isolated to user-centric identity models reflects an ongoing effort to reduce reliance on centralized authorities while improving user control and interoperability. However, even user-centric models continue to depend on trusted intermediaries such as identity providers. Self-Sovereign Identity emerges as a further evolution that aims to eliminate this dependency by enabling decentralized identity management through cryptographic mechanisms and distributed trust infrastructures. This section presents the core principles, components, and architectural foundations of self-sovereign identity.

This dissertation positions SSI not merely as an alternative model but as a paradigm shift in digital identity management. Unlike legacy IAM systems, SSI enables decentralized trust and empowers individuals to assert and manage their identities independently.

The *Self-Sovereign Identity* is the next step in the continuum along the lines of the centralized model and federated identity models. While SSI has been gaining recognition in recent years [57][58][59], it has its privacy roots in the in 1970's by the introduction of Diffie-Hellman key exchange protocol that allows users to protect their privacy in the digital environment using public-key cryptography [60].

The term Self-Sovereign Identity originated from a blog post in 2012 by Devon Lofretto to the Vendor Relationship Management (VRM) mailing list with the title 'Sovereign Source Authority' [61].

Also known as *self-managed identity*, and *user-controlled identity*, SSI is an identity management model in which the *identity holder* has broader control over their data and decides how and under what conditions their data should be shared with others. The SSI model is intended to preserve the right for the selective disclosure of the identity holder's data in different contexts. The identity holder is a role an entity might perform by possessing one or more claims. An identity holder is not always the subject of claims they are holding.

In SSI literature, several roles are distinguished. An entity refers to any participant in the identity ecosystem. A holder is an entity that possesses credentials. An issuer creates credentials, and a verifier validates them. In this dissertation, the term user refers to a human entity acting as a credential holder.

In [2] Christopher Allen defines SSI as follows:

> "...The user must be central to the administration of identity. That requires not just the interoperability of a user's identity across multiple locations, with the user's consent, but also true user control of that digital identity, creating user autonomy. To accomplish this, a self-sovereign identity must be transportable; it can't be locked down to one site or locale. A self-sovereign identity must also allow ordinary users to make claims, which could include personally identifying information or facts about personal capability or group membership. It can even contain information about the user that was asserted by other persons or groups."

Allen provides the following ten principles defining an SSI system [2]:

- *Existence:* "Users must have an independent existence."

- *Control:* "Users must control their identities." They should have the liberty to manage their attributes in any way desired as they have complete authority over their identity data. Note that this does not stop entities from making claims about other entities. Also there should be a distinction between identifiers and identities. Identifiers must be managed by the user themselves. There should also be a distinction between control and ownership of the data. A user may possess control over an identity claim issued to them, but they may not be the owner of that claim. For example a driver's license number is issued by the government and can be revoked by the government. However the user should have the ability to control and share their driver's license number under their conditions.

- *Access:* "Users must have access to their own data." There must be no gatekeepers or filters without the knowledge and approval of the identity owner. Note this does not infer that any identity holder can modify all of the claims associated with their identity, but rather it means they should be aware of such actions. Moreover, this principle applies to every entity with respect to their own identity, and not to other's.

- *Transparency:* "Systems and algorithms must be transparent." The algorithms, procedures, and processes involved in the model should be visible to the identity holders. Free, well-known, and open-source frameworks are a logical solution to this criterion, opening the algorithms to public examinations, evaluation, and avoiding vendor lock-ins.

- *Persistence:* "Identities must be long-lived." Identity data should be long-lived and persistent until they are explicitly decommissioned by the identity holder. Note that identity formation is an ongoing process and every identity management model must be designed to be adequately flexible to allow the identity holders to obtain, modify or remove their identity data. For example, a person's name and address may change throughout their life. This does not mean that an identity holder controls all of the claims on their identity: other entities may make claims about the identity holder, but they should not be central to the identity themselves.

- *Portability:* "Information and services about identity must be transportable." The identity holder should have the ability to seamlessly transport its identity data from one location to another. This is a necessary process for the longevity of the identity data. The identity data should not be locked into a single third-party entity if the third-party service provider has the best intentions of the identity holder.

- *Interoperability:* "Identities should be as widely usable as possible." The identity data should be usable by as many entities as possible. The identity data should be consumable by a range of entities from different boundaries, jurisdictions, and architectures. This criterion supports the availability and durability of identity attributes.

- *Consent:* "Users must agree to the use of their identity." The identity holder should have a clear understanding and provide their approval on how their identity data is used.

- *Minimization:* "Disclosure of claims must be minimized." The least amount of identity data must be disclosed to accomplish the task at hand. This requirement is supported through the use of selective disclosure, range proofs, and other privacy preserving techniques to ensure only the necessary data is disclosed.

- *Protection:* "The rights of users must be protected." The SSI model places identity holders in the center of its architecture. The right of identity holders must be preserved at all times. In cases where there is a conflict between the identity holder and the network, the network should err on the side of preserving the rights of the identity holder. Moreover, SSI architecture should be orchestrated in a decentralized form to avoid possible censorship and monopolies.

To avoid confusion, the distinction between the terms identity owners and identity holder in the context of SSI must be stated. An identity owner is an entity, such as a user, an organization, or a machine, that owns and issues a set of claims. On the other hand, an identity holder is an entity that holds in their possession one or more claims, and may not necessary be the owner of those claims.

The SSI model has been proposed as a step towards solving the challenges found in traditional identity management models. While the scholarly work around SSI is rapidly growing, many major aspects of design and implementation of SSI are taking place in the technical communities by means of discussions, projects, presentations, and whitepapers.

In the book "Self-Sovereign Identity: Decentralized digital identity and verifiable credential", authors provide a comprehensive definition of SSI, its building blocks, and its governance framework [62].

In the book "Digital Identity Crisis", Rooly Eliezerov discusses the value of data and approaches to digital identity. He further elaborates on the key challenges of current digital identity models and the benefits of the SSI model[63]. S. Fedrous et al. [9] provide a survey of definition and analysis on SSI.

While growing rapidly, the SSI model has many challenges needing to be answered. Addressing these challenges accelerates its rate of adoption and use.

Challenges of Self-Sovereign Identity

Self-Sovereign Identity model is considered as the latest evolution of IAM models. SSI attempts to address a number of shortcomings found in the existing digital identity space. However, it also produces a unique set of challenges that warrant adequate research, exploration, and discussion. The following paragraphs discuss these challenges:

- *Standards for Data Management and Wallets:* Standard protocols, practices, and policies around user experience, data management, and data exchange should be carefully defined and implemented. While SSI supports an open ecosystem, there is value in consistent yet flexible user interactions, data management policies, and data presentation standards. Regardless of the direction taken to address this challenge, the approach should aim for a user-centric system aligned with Privacy by Design and Security by Design principles. The principles of Privacy by Design are described in section 7.

- *Key Management:* In traditional identity management models, the identity providers are primarily responsible for the management of identity data and secret keys, and therefore must address the liabilities, risks, and technical requirements associated with that task. Conversely, in the SSI model this responsibility, and its associated risks, are placed on the shoulders of the users. There have been numerous instances of users losing their cryptographic keys, resulting in the loss of valuable information and unrecoverable funds. Addressing the key management requirements in the SSI architecture is a fundamental step towards the mass adoption of SSI. Reliance on decentralized key custodians is one form of addressing the key management challenge [64].

- *Consent:* As stated by Article 4 of General Data Protection Regulation (GDPR)[65], the consent given by the user must be meaningful, well-formed, unambiguous, specific, and freely given, specifying clear decisions. This process is not easy to implement and hard to verify in the current identity models. Moreover, requesting users to provide consent to many privacy policies and data sharing practices has led to what is known as *consent fatigue*, where the user is bombarded with privacy notifications. Ideas such as automated decision making and response by digital wallets or agents representing the user, based on prior user decisions, should be entertained. Moreover, research around consent management, presentation, and enforcement is valuable.

- *Access:* Some SSI implementations rely on decentralized ledger technologies (DLT) as verifiable data registries. The concept of DLT and blockchain will be explained in the next sections. Certain DLT systems are public, allowing any entity to read or write to the ledger, while others are permissioned and allow only a selection of authorized entities to read or write new records into the ledger. If not carefully designed, the permissioned approach possesses the risk of forming centralized architecture similar to an oligopoly among the few authorized entities [66]. On the other hand, the permission-less and public model may be vulnerable to attacks common in various open DLT architectures [8].

- *Accountability and Governance:* It is important to articulate the policies and procedures around identifying and addressing malicious behavior and dishonest entities. It is also important to realize and articulate the correct degree of decentralization needed to support the vision and the requirements of SSI. Certain identity management operations such as identity claim issuance, identity lookup, and secure storage of data may rely on some degree of centralization and dependence on trusted intermediaries. Some implementations of SSI place significant power in the hands of a select few trusted entities that must comply with a common contractually-binding trust framework, potentially making these entities the weakest point of the network. While other implementations of SSI aim for a more decentralized, programmable, and machine-readable governance framework. The latter form of governance too has shown to suffer from various flaws in the past [67]. Therefore, efforts to determine the correct balance between centralization and decentralization is an important topic.

- *Trust in Data:* While there may be trust in the underlying SSI network as a secure, robust, and decentralized platform, the methods to form trust among the entities, and the trust in data including the verifiable credentials exchanged must be carefully designed. The authentication and data validation may need to be done through a trusted authority and outside of the blockchain network.

- *New Technology Adoption:* As a new identity model, SSI requires various modifications to the existing system architectures. An important step towards the success of

SSI is the discussions around the suitable technology stacks, deployment practices, and operational procedures. Particular attention must be given to the user experience, including the user interactions from the operator's perspective. Proper design steps must be taken to avoid the fate experienced by many other good innovations such as Pretty Good Privacy (PGP) [68], which while is a useful technology it has not met the expected broad use.

- *Investment and Commercialization:* As a relatively new venture with a growing ecosystem but with limited knowledge on the revenue model, unknown user acceptance and utilization and unknown risks, any entity intending to adopt SSI must design a strategic plan that supports the investment and risk involved in the deployment and operation of such system. The SSI economic model may lead to the chicken and egg problem where user adoption depends on the support of the service providers and vice versa.

An adequate response to the aforementioned challenges is the premise for a strong acceptance and support of the SSI model. Section **??** provides more perspective on existing SSI challenges.

In the next section, we delve deeper into the architecture of SSI and explain its building blocks.

2.4.1 The Architecture of Self-Sovereign Identity Model

While prior identity models depend on centralized trust anchors, SSI introduces decentralized identifiers (DIDs), verifiable credentials (VCs), and registries as foundational primitives.

These innovations address critical issues such as selective disclosure, trust minimization, and credential portability. In this dissertation, we evaluate and extend these architectural elements to support scalable, privacy-enhancing identity operations across diverse application domains.

Decentralized Identifiers

Developed by World Wide Web Consortium (W3C) [69], The Decentralized Identifiers (DID) [70] are a key component of SSI model. The DID specification defines a globally unique and cryptographic identifier scheme similar to the Universally Unique Identifier scheme (UUID) [71] with a number of differences. First, the DID specification does not rely on a centralized authority to manage the identifiers (hence called Decentralized Identifiers), but rather they can be managed using a decentralized infrastructure such as DLT. Second, the DID addresses have cryptographic properties. The DID addresses are generated based on cryptographic key pairs. The ownership of a DID can be proven using cryptographic proofs such as digital signatures. As shown in Figure 2.8 a DID address consists of three parts. Every DID has the following format:

<Scheme>:<Method>:<Method Specific Identifier>.

The first part of each DID is the DID Scheme, followed by the DID Method. The third part consists of an identifier in the context of a DID Method. Each DID address resolves to a *DID Descriptor object* or DDO. Also known as a *DID Document.* A DDO is a machine-readable JSON-LD[72] document with various information about the DID subject. These include cryptographic public keys, service endpoints, authentication parameters, timestamps and other metadata. The service endpoints provide a publicly available address for establishing connection with the DID subject. A *DID subject* is an entity identified by a DID and described by a DDO. A *DID record* consist of a key-value pair of a DID and a DDO. Figure 2.8 depicts a sample DDO document. An entity may have multiple key pairs and DIDs, and use a different DID for each interaction.

The *DID Method* defines the specific methods a DID scheme can be implemented on a particular DLT or network. This includes the CRUD operations of creating, reading, update and deleting of DID records. As of now there are 90 registered DID methods [73]. These methods include Bitcoin, Ethereum, Sovrin, Interplanetary File System (IPFS) [74] and

```
did:example:123456789abcdefghi
```


```
{
  "@context": "https://w3id.org/did/v1",
  "id": "did:example:123456789abcdefghi",

  "publicKey": [
    {
      "id": "did:example:123456789abcdefghi#keys-1",
      "type": "RsaVerificationKey2018",
      "owner": "did:example:123456789abcdefghi",
      "publicKeyPem": "Public key goes here..."
    }
  ],

  "authentication": [
    {
      "type": "RsaSignatureAuthentication2018",
      "publicKey": "did:example:123456789abcdefghi#keys-1"
    }
  ],

  "service": [
    {
      "type": "ExampleService",
      "serviceEndpoint": "https://example.com/endpoint/8377464"
    }
  ]
}
```


Figure 2.8: Sample decentralized identifier (DID) and DID Document (DDO)

Veres Ones [75].

The DID specification distinguishes three types of DID [76]. The *Anywise DID* or *Public DID* is a DID intended for use with an unknown-able number of parties. The *Pairwise DID* is intended for interactions where the DID should only be known by its subject and exactly one other entity such as a service provider. Lastly, the *N-wise DID* is intended to be known by exactly N number of entity including its subject.

A *Universal Resolver* [77] is a DID resolving system that supports multiple decentralized identifier systems. For a DID system to support the universal resolver it must implement a DID adaptor to interface the universal resolver with the system specific DID methods.

The *DID Auth* protocol allows an identity owner to use their client application, such as

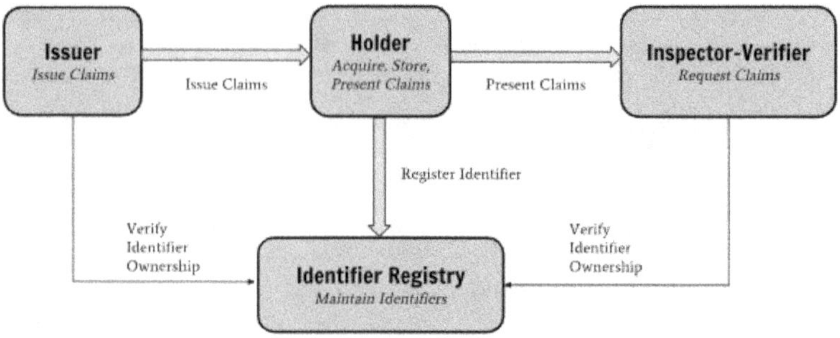

Figure 2.9: Verifiable Credentials Actors

their mobile device or browser, to prove to a service provider that they are in control of a DID. DID Auth protocol relies on a challenge-response cycle that is customized depending on the situation. This protocol can replace the use of username and passwords as a form of authentication and enables an authenticated communication channel between an identity owner and a service provider.

DIDComm is a DID-based communication protocol that enables two or more SSI entities to exchange messages securely and privately in a peer-to-peer manner. The protocol relies on DIDs for endpoint discovery and cryptographic key resolution, and supports mutual authentication between communicating parties without requiring centralized intermediaries [78].

Verifiable Credentials

The *Verifiable Credentials (VC)* [32] is a specification developed by W3C Verifiable Credentials working group. A verifiable credential is an interoperable data structure suitable for representing cryptographically verifiable and tamper-proof claims. Figure 2.9 obtained from [32] displays the key roles within the verifiable credentials' ecosystem.

As stated before, a *holder* is an entity that controls one or more verifiable credentials. An *issuer* is an entity that creates new verifiable credentials. A bank and a government agency are examples of credential issuers. A *verifier* is an entity that obtains one more verifiable credentials to verify. An e-commerce website expecting credentials from their customers is an example of a verifier. A *verifiable data registry* is responsible for mediating the creation and verification of identifiers, keys, verifiable credentials schemas and other relevant data required to use verifiable credentials. A verifiable credential consists of various elements. They include the URI of the subject, the URI of the issuer of the claims, and the URIs that uniquely identify the credential. In addition, a VC include claim expiration conditions and cryptographic signatures. A URI can be a DID. The W3C Verifiable Credentials working group has also defined the concept of *Verifiable Presentations (VP)*. Verifiable presentations define the methods by which VCs are signed and presented by the holder. A VC or a VP can be described with JSON-LD, JSON [79], or JSON Web Token [80].

Decentralized Public Key Infrastructure

The Public Key Infrastructure consists of a set of services, tools, processes, and technologies which facilitate the performance of cryptographic operations based on public key cryptography. The most commonly used PKI certificate model is known as PKI X.509 or PKIX. In this model, the central certificate authorities (CA) create the X.509 digital certificate. A certificate binds a public key to a particular identity [81]. Along with certificate authorities, the Domain Name Server (DNS) registrars and Internet Corporation for Assigned Names and Numbers (ICANN) [82] were created to facilitate the management and resolution of online identifiers and addresses. The governance model utilized by the above central authorities runs the risk of placing the control of identity data and decision making in the hands of a small set of central authorities, leading to the possibility for those authorities to misbehave or become victims of security breaches [83]. Recent development in the formation of the Post-Transition IANA (PTI) entity as part of the transition stewardship program within ICANN, to perform the responsibilities of Assigned Numbers Authority's (IANA)

[84][85] , and other advancement in introducing broader community driven decision making within ICANN have brought forth the hope of better accountability and democratic decision making in this space [86].

A well-known implementation of a decentralized trust model, before the emergence of blockchain is the Pretty Good Privacy protocol. Proposed by Phil Zimmermann, and contrary to traditional PKI models, the PGP trust model relies on on *a web of trust.* The popularity and growth of PGP were inhibited by various unanswered usability and key management challenges [83] in addition to the security concerns associated with the use of long term keys.

Proposed by the Rebooting of the Web of Trust (RWoT) [87], the *Decentralized Public Key infrastructure (DPKI)* provides a decentralized trust architecture in which no single entity can compromise the security and integrity of the system as a whole [45]. In contrast to traditional PKI, the DPKI does not depend on central certificate authorities or registration authorities (RA). The dependence from these central entities can be eliminated by relying on a decentralized platform as the initial root of trust.

The DPKI architecture can be realized with the help of a decentralized key-value data store such as blockchain. By relying on the immutability of the blockchain to store the public keys, it is possible to guarantee that the data cannot be deleted or modified by anyone once it is written. The cryptographic keys can be found by anyone who has access to blockchain. No CA is not responsible for their storage or verification. This addresses some of the privacy and security concerns associated with a central point of authority. Because of the transparent and open nature of public blockchains, any changes to the data is auditable by all members of the network. Note, we must distinguish the trust placed on the blockchain system as a transparent, immutable and secure storage platform, and the trust placed in the data itself, such as the public keys stored on the blockchain. While a verifier can rely on DPKI to allow a particular entity to authenticate itself and claim the possession of a particular identifier and public key, that does not translate to the verifier trusting the entity's identity. The identification of an entity is achieved through the exchange of verifiable credentials. Although verifiable credentials contain digitally signed identity claims, ultimately it is up to the verifier to trust and accept or reject those claims based on its own policies and trust model.

The Sidetree project proposed through Decentralized Identity Foundation (DIF) [88] is an emerging protocol for creating scalable DPKI networks that can run on top of any existing decentralized anchoring system such as Bitcoin, while being as open and public as the underlying system they utilize [89]. Sivakumar and Singh [90] developed a blockchain-based DPKI by which key management operations are addressed through the use of smart contracts.

It is important to note that not all security breaches and concerns around traditional PKI are due to its fundamental architecture, but rather because of inadequate enforcement of security controls in a PKI deployment, or the lack of proper key management by users who engage with the system. Similar issues can be found in DPKI models which offer high data resiliency but can be vulnerable to various attacks. Because of the role the CA plays, popular public CAs have adopted high levels of operational security and go to a great length to protect sensitive data. Decentralized PKI systems must also follow strict security measures. While some aspect of DPKI may rely on blockchain, many tasks such as cryptographic signing operations require secret keys which must be performed in a secure, central and off the blockchain environment.

In addition, while DPKI systems offer a transparent and open architecture, the CAs in the traditional PKI model have also taken steps towards better transparency by offering services such as certificate transparency logs [91], through which all issued certificates are published on the CAs website.

Many PKI enterprise systems have been deployed in various industries including banking, health and defense. Due to the rapid growth of PKI ecosystem, deployment and management of PKI systems have become easier. There are now many on-premise and cloud based PKI options available in the industry. For private ecosystems where certificate issuance and renovation detail of the parties must remain private, the cost of deploying a private DPKI with a large number of nodes may not be financially feasible.

Blockchain and Distributed Ledger Technology

The blockchain technology and its super-set the Distributed Ledger Technology (DLT) provide a cryptographically secure, decentralized, and distributed database of information. The blockchain underpins the vast majority of cryptocurrencies, such as Bitcoin [8]. The blockchain dis-intermediates the central authorities, allowing the transactions to take place in a peer-to-peer method without the reliance on a trusted central party. Certain blockchain implementations such as Ethereum [25] support *smart contracts* capabilities. Smart contracts are distributed applications executed by the participating blockchain nodes.

The applications of blockchain have surpassed beyond the financial use cases and grown into other industries such as Internet of Things, smart homes, health care, supply chain management, energy, legal, voting, storage, corporate registry, as well as identity management. As the most well known form of DLT, the blockchain technology became known after the introduction of the Bitcoin white-paper in October of 2008 by a person, or persons of the name Satoshi Nakamoto. The Bitcoin protocol was officially launched on the third of January 2009. Bitcoin is by far the most well known and longest running application of blockchain technology.

A blockchain system consists of an immutable ledger of cryptographically hashed transactions. A group of transactions collected together forms a block. Each block contains a header that references the cryptographic hash of the previous block in the blockchain. Figure 2.10 represents a chain of blocks, where each block references the block before it. Weichao Gao *et al.* [92] provide a comprehensive description of the blockchain system, its major components, algorithms, and challenges.

Blockchain systems can be divided into two categories of public and private, and two

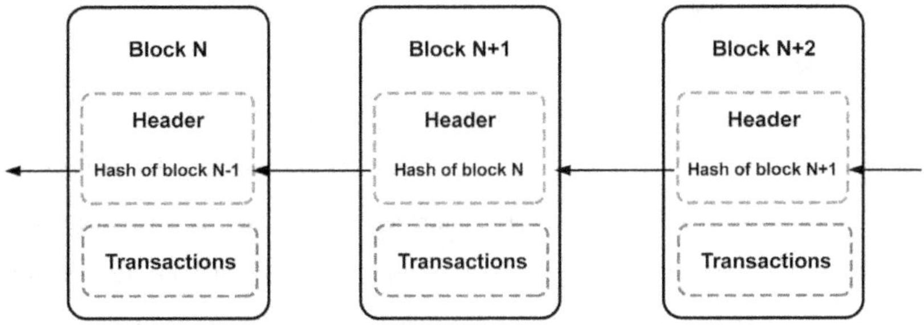

Figure 2.10: Blocks in the Blockchain architecture

types of permissioned and permission-less. A public blockchain is completely available to all public members to read, while a private blockchain is accessible only to the authorized entities. Being a public network, PII information are generally not added to these systems. A permissioned blockchain provides read access to all parties, however, writing permission is only granted to a subset of entities. Conversely a permission-less blockchain allows for anyone to write to the blockchain. Bitcoin and Ethereum are examples of public permission-less blockchains as they are open to the everyone to read or write. Hyperledger Fabric [93] is a popular private blockchain, while Hyperledger Indy [94] is an instance of a public permissioned DLT.

The consensus protocol is an integral component of blockchain. It ensures that only valid transactions are added to the blockchain. There are a large number of consensus algorithms [95] available. These algorithms date back to 1982 with the introduction of a paper by Leslie Lamport *et al.* describing the challenges and solutions of reaching Byzantine Fault Tolerance (BFT) [96]. While the consensus among known parties may be achieved through BFT and its variants, public blockchains such as Bitcoin where participants are not trusted must rely on other classes of consensus algorithms. Bitcoin relies on a consensus protocol known as *proof-of-work*. In this protocol, the participants of the network are required to solve a difficult mathematical puzzle in order to prove the validity of the transactions they intend to submit to the network. L.M. Back et al. [97] and Du Mingxiao et al. [98] provide a comprehensive overview and comparative analysis among various consensus algorithms.

Blockchain provides a framework of trust, and the opportunity for data storage and processing to be diffused among numerous entities. By leveraging this architecture, the need for the continuous availability of a central identity providers may no longer be necessary.

The advantages of using blockchain to achieve IAM requirements are four folds. First, the decentralized nature of blockchain allows data and decentralized identifiers to be stored in a ledger and not with a single central entity. Second, as blockchain is an immutable, the transactions can only be appended to the ledger and its integrity can be verified by all members of the network.

Third, in the case of a public blockchains, all records are always visible to all.

Finally, due to the distributed nature of blockchain, it is very difficult to influence the availability and integrity of the data.

Various types of operations such as registration of decentralized identifiers, notarization of identity data, and storage of access and consent records can be shared on blockchain. The decentralized nature of the blockchain allows for entity identifiers and cryptographic keys to be registered on an immutable, decentralized system accessible by any entities that need to obtain the authentic public key of an identifier. This is in contrast to the public key infrastructure, where the public keys are exchanged directly through a presumably secure channel, with strong dependence on certificate authorities to ensure the integrity and authenticity of the public keys. In more recent SSI architectures various information such as entity identifiers are no longer added to the blockchain system, as they are considered PII information. Furthermore, by leveraging smart contracts on blockchain it is possible to develop sophisticated and decentralized identity management platforms on the blockchain.

As discussed previously, while a blockchain system provides integrity, immutability, and authenticity of cryptographic keys, it fails to prove the trustworthiness of cryptographic keys without the existence of a proper identity layer, governance framework and trust policy in place. Moreover, in the context of public blockchains, privacy concerns around identity data, and issues around data correlation are important topics of discussion.

Verifiable Data Registry

The goals of SSI can be realized with the help of a trusted database platform such as a blockchain playing the role of a *Verifiable Data Registry*. A verifiable data registry is responsible for mediating the creation and verification of identifiers, keys, verifiable credentials schemas, revocation registries, issuers' public keys and other relevant data required to generate or use verifiable credentials. Note that other forms of databases, such as government ID database can also be considered as a Verifiable Data Registry. There can also be more than one type of registry utilized in an SSI deployment.

Agents

An agent is a piece of software component assigned to act on behalf of an entity. [99]. Agents serve a multitude of purposes. In the context of an SSI network, an agent is the main gateway between an entity and the rest of the network by providing a network address for other entities to connect through. Generally, an agent component has access to a digital wallet in order to store cryptographic keys and to perform various cryptographic operations. The agent component ensures resource availability, increased privacy, and auditing capability. In addition, it provides effective data management services and supports automated actions on behalf of the user. The drawbacks of agents include the trust placed in them to handle sensitive data on behalf of the entity [66].

There are two broad categories of agents, namely *edge agents* and *cloud agents* [100]. An edge agent is an agent service running in the immediate vicinity of the user. This includes the user's mobile device or browser. The edge agent interacts directly with the user and has the ability to provide more direct and immediate data control to its user. An edge agent is required to be available at all times in order to respond to any service requests. A cloud agent, on the other hand, is an agent service hosted on the cloud. Generally, a cloud agent has more restrictive access policies than an edge agent. Generally, a cloud agent has a fixed and public address, making it susceptible against identification through correlation attacks. The cloud agent is capable of relaying all requests to its associated edge agent running on the user's device. Service providers that provide cloud-based agents as a service are called *agencies*.

Various efforts in standardizing the agent's interface and communication protocol are underway [101]. Smart or AI agents are advanced agents with the ability to respond to various requests with minimal user involvement. Smart agents can be equipped with artificial intelligence to improve their decision-making capabilities. Google Assistant and other smart devices can enhance the user experience of agents [102].

Identity Hubs

Proposed by Decentralized Identity Foundation [103] an *Identity Hub* is a secure data storage solution that provides a safe, highly available, and user centric depository of user data. Identity hubs support interoperable and standard protocols for effective management and exchange of identity data and cryptographic information. Identity hubs support synchronization protocols to coordinate user data among multiple hubs; and are required to support data exportation capabilities to allow the user's data to be exported in an interoperable format at the user's request. Authentication with an identity hub is supported through various protocols such as DID Authentication scheme. An alternative yet similar solution to secure storage of identity data is known as the Solid Project [104]. Solid provides a decentralized data store called a Pod - similar to a container - for storing identity data of the users. They support file and graph based data structures and can be hosted by a Pod provider or by the user themselves. As of now there are four Pod providers. The Solid project supports OpenID as its main authentication protocol.

Digital Wallets

A digital wallet is a software or hardware component responsible for the storage of identity data and cryptographic keys in a secure and privacy-respecting method. In addition, often in concert with an agent, a wallet can perform various cryptographic operations such as key generation, signature creation, signature verification, and key backup and recovery. In order to comply with existing privacy and auditing requirements, a wallet may support the tracking of consent requests and responses, as well as all user interactions. A digital wallet can be deployed in many forms. It can be a program on the user's mobile device or browser or provided as a software as a service via the cloud. Lastly, a user may have multiple wallets.

These architectural components form the technical foundation upon which the novel mechanisms proposed in this dissertation are built.

2.5 Privacy Engineering

While SSI provides a decentralized architecture for identity management, many of its privacy guarantees rely on advanced cryptographic primitives. These techniques enable properties such as selective disclosure, anonymous authentication, and secure multi-party verification without exposing sensitive personal data. The following section reviews several privacy engineering techniques that complement SSI systems.

Privacy engineering covers the tools, processes, techniques, metrics, and taxonomy to implement Privacy by Design. It ensures that privacy considerations are integrated into the system design. NIST defines privacy engineering as "A specialty discipline of systems engineering focused on achieving freedom from conditions that can create problems for individuals with unacceptable consequences that arise from the system as it processes PII" [105].

Privacy engineering can supplement and extend SSI by addressing various critical requirements such as consent and data minimization. Because privacy engineering is vast and rapidly evolving field, this section only describes a selection of highly discussed topics including Trusted Execution Environments, Secure Multi-Party Computation protocols and Ring Signatures, Threshold Secret Sharing, and Zero Knowledge Proofs protocols.

2.5.1 Trusted Execution Environments

Smartphone ownership is accelerating globally along with the growth of their capabilities and the ability to run more applications. This contributes to the increasing number of smartphone vulnerabilities. Trusted Execution Environment (TEE) can provide a method of protecting mobile applications and user's data from unauthorized access. Digital wallets and agents play a vital role in SSI architecture. The wallet must securely store user's cryptographic keys and identity attributes. Wallets can leverage TEE to maintain data confidentiality and secure code execution. Trusted Execution Environment is a tamper-resistant, secure, and protected processing enclave inside a processor that runs in parallel, but isolated, to the main operating system running on the device [106]. A TEE component provides an enhanced level of code and data confidentiality and authenticity of executed code, and the integrity of the run-time states. Applications that run in a TEE zone have access to the full features of the device, however, they are isolated at the hardware level from the user-installed applications running on the main operating system. Intel's SGX, AMD SEV, and ARM's TrustZone are popular examples of TEE.

2.5.2 Threshold Signatures, Secure Multi-Party Computation and Ring Signatures

Ring Signature is a privacy respecting digital signature protocol that provides the ability to prove the existence of a signer that possesses the signing key among a group of signers without revealing the signer's public key. Ring signatures make it possible to produce a valid signature without revealing the identity of the signer [107]. Ring Signatures and

Secure Multi-party Computation (SMC) [108] supplement the SSI architecture by enabling joint computations while maintaining data confidentiality. They also allow for retaining more control over who receives the outcome of the computation.

Secure Multi-party Computation provides a privacy-preserving method for a group of entities to jointly compute a function over their input without the need to share their input with other parties, or with a trusted third party. A trusted third party is an entity trusted by other entities within a particular context. As an example, assuming there are three parties Alice, Charlie, and Bob with secret inputs x, y, and z representing their respective salaries. To find out the highest of the three salaries without revealing to each other their salary, they engage in an MPC protocol. The output of the protocol is simply the highest value of the salaries which can then be used by each party to compare against. Mathematically, the problem of finding the maximum value translates to $F(x, y, z) = max(x, y, z)$.

Threshold Secret Sharing and secret segmentation refer to the distribution of secrets into multiple shares. These shares are then disclosed with multiple participants. To recover the secret, a pre-determined number of shares must be retrieved from the participants. More formally, given a finite set P of participants and a set Γ of subsets of P, the secret threshold scheme defines a threshold t where the secret access model is $\Gamma = \{A \subseteq P : |A| \geq t\}$. In these schemes less than t participants cannot recover the original secret. This scheme is also known as the (t, n) - threshold scheme.

The SSI architecture can take advantage of Threshold Secret Sharing protocol to offer secure and privacy respecting backup and recovery of user's sensitive data, including secret keys [109].

History of secure multi-party computation begins in 1986 when Yao proposed the two-party computation protocol using cryptography [108]. Goldreich et al. [110] extended Yao's idea by providing a polynomial-time algorithm to solve the multi-party (mental game) problem under the assumption of the majority of parties being honest.

Various applications of SMC have since been introduced, such as the private information retrieval (PIR) problem [111]. PIR describes a server-client architecture where a client retrieves the ith bit of a binary sequence from the server without the server knowing which bit was retrieved. At the same time, the client does not gain access to the entire binary sequence. Another application is privacy-preserving data mining.

For example, Lindell and Pinkas [112] propose an approach where two parties, each with separate databases, jointly perform data mining operations on the union of their datasets without disclosing their databases to each other or a third party.

Nair et al. [113] propose a secure information storage and retrieval model based on SMC, relying on Shamir's secret sharing [114] to split sensitive data among multiple databases. Data reconstruction is performed by a computation agent on the client side.

Clifton et al. [115] describe a toolkit for privacy-preserving SMC-based data mining operations, including secure sum computation using a secret random number. However, in this protocol, two adjacent parties can collude to compute the random number. To address this, Sheikh et al. [116] propose a privacy-preserving k-secure sum protocol that segments each partys data and generates random numbers within each segment to prevent collusion.

Pathak et al. [117] extend this work by proposing a secure and privacy-preserving data mining protocol. Each party breaks its data block into k segments and distributes $k - 1$ segments to other parties. Through a series of interchanges, the total sum of the data is calculated while maintaining the privacy of individual data.

Pinkas [118] provides a comprehensive discussion of SMC and various privacy-preserving data mining techniques.

An early example of multi-party sharing for RSA signatures was proposed by Santis et al. [119]. Secret threshold sharing and segmentation involve distributing secrets into multiple shares, which are then shared among participants. To recover the secret, a predetermined number of shares must be retrieved.

Formally, given a finite set P of participants and a set Γ of subsets of P, the secret threshold scheme defines a threshold t where the secret access model is $\Gamma = \{A \subseteq P :$

$|A| \geq t\}$. In these schemes fewer than t participants cannot recover the original secret.

In 1979, Shamir [114] and Blakely [120] proposed two variations of threshold-based secret sharing schemes. Shamir's scheme relies on standard Lagrange polynomial interpolation, while Blakely's vector scheme uses the geometric concept of intersecting hyperplanes. An evaluation of these approaches is discussed in [121].

Shamir's secret sharing algorithm is described as follows: User V splits a secret S into P shares, such that any combination of less than t shares cannot learn the secret S , while any combination of $\geq t$ shares can learn the secret S. To this end the user V constructs a polynomial f of degree $t-1$ such that $f(0) = S$. For example if at least 4 shares are required to reconstruct S then the polynomial will be $f(x) = a_0 + a_1x + a_2x^2 + a_3x^3$. Next, user V computes $f(x_i)$ for all shares $i \subseteq P$ and the resulting pairs $\{x_i, f(x_i)\}$ are distributed to each participant i. In order to reconstruct the secret S the polynomial $f(x)$ should be recreated from the set of pairs provided by the participants using Lagrange Polynomial Interpolation. The major steps of Lagrange Interpolation are as follows: Given a polynomial $f(x)$ over of degree at most l, and given C such that$|C| = l + 1$, then

$$f(x) = \sum_{i \in C} f(i)\delta_i(x)$$

where $\delta_i(x)$ is a degree l polynomial such that

$$\delta_i(j) = \begin{cases} 0 & \text{if } i \neq j \\ 1 & \text{if } i = j \end{cases}$$

which can also be represented as

$$\delta_i(j) = \prod_{j \in C, j \neq i} \frac{X - j}{i - j}$$

Sun et al. [122] propose a key recovery model where the user's cryptographic key is divided into fragments. Each fragment is encrypted using a private key derived from the master key and sent to different key escrow providers. To recover the keys, the fragments are retrieved and decrypted using the master key.

2.5.3 Zero Knowledge Proofs

Zero Knowledge Proof (ZKP) is a cryptographic protocol by which a *prover* is able to, with high certainty, prove the validity of a statement to a *verifier* without sharing the underlying information [123]. The prover is able to maintain its privacy while providing to the verifier enough information to be able to validate the truthfulness of a statement. The ZKP protocol enhances user privacy while maintaining the required institutional trust for the correctness of digital interactions.

ZKP protocols are used in various applications including privacy respecting identity proving and authentication, as well as cryptocurrency transaction validation and private data mining.

ZKP augments SSI's data minimization requirements and empowers users by impeding the unnecessary collection of their data by a verifier. In the context of verifiable credentials, ZKP introduces the following key capabilities [32]:

- The ability to combine multiple VC from multiple issuers into a single verifiable presentation while avoiding sharing unnecessary VC or identifiers with the verifier, making it more challenging for the verifier to collude with any of the issuers
- The ability to selectively disclose the necessary claims with a verifiable credential to a verifier without requiring the need to obtain multiple atomic VC from the issuers. This allows the holder to only share the information needed by the verifier
- The possibility to produce derived verifiable credentials formatted according to the verifier's data schema, without the involvement of the issuer

As an example, a prover is able to prove to a verifier that he is above the age of 19 without revealing his actual date of birth, or a prover can prove that she lives in a country within the European Union without revealing the name of the country.

Zero Knowledge Proofs were first published by S. Goldwasser et al. in 1985 [123]. After 27 years from the time the paper was published, Goldwasser et al. won the Turing award for their effort in ZKP.

A simplified form of ZKP is the public key cryptography, where the possession of a private key is proven by a challenge-response protocol. Notable works are Succinct ZK by Joe Kilian in 1992 [124] which provides a simplified ZKP, and Pinocchio by B. Parno et al. in 2013 which applies ZKP to real-life use cases [125], as well as J. Groths's Groth16 proposed in 2016 [126], which significantly reduces the protocol's computational complexity. The Bulletproofs protocol by B. Bunz et al. [127] has contributed significantly to the progress of ZKP. Other notable ZKP protocols include CL-signatures [128], Fiat Shamir [129], zkSNARKs [130] and zkSTARKs [131]. IBM Identity Mixer [132] and Microsoft U-Prove [133] are also among discussed ZKP implementations.

Zero Knowledge Proofs belong to a broader class of cryptographic proof systems. Proof systems can be divided into interactive and non-interactive proof systems (NIPS). An interactive ZKP requires the prover and verifier to be present during the verification process through which multiple messages are exchanged between the parties. At the end of this process, the verifier will either accept or reject the proof provided by the prover. The exchange between the parties requires an active connection. Conversely, the non-interactive proof systems, first introduced by Blum *et al.* [134] do not require the concurrent availability of both parties. Huixin Wu et al. provide a survey of non-interactive ZKP systems and their applications [135].

Every ZKP protocol must satisfy these three principal properties:

- *Completeness:* If the input to a ZKP system is true, the proof must also be true. In other words, referring to the example above, if the date of birth attribute meets the condition of, greater than 19 years, then the result of the system received by the verifier must be accepted (with high probability) as true.

- *Soundness:* If the input to the ZKP system is false, then the proof must also be false. In other words, it is not possible for the prover to trick the system to convince the verifier when the input is false.

- *Privacy:* The confidential input of the ZKP system must not be revealed to parties other than the prover

There are a number of canonical examples illustrating ZKP protocol, including the Ali Baba's cave [136], and the two pens scenario [137].

A ZKP ecosystem consists of various roles and terminologies, which are described as follows:

- *Attributes* are units of information about the identity holder. Date of birth or nationality are examples of attributes.

- *Holder* as stated before, the holder is the entity who possesses the attributes. These attributes are attested by one or more authoritative sources, also known as the issuer. The holder uses the attributes to generate proofs to prove some claims about the attributes.

- *Issuer* is the authoritative party that attests to the validity of the holder's attributes. For example, a government agency may issue a certified date of birth attribute to the holder.

- *Verifier* is the party that verifies the claims, by verifying the proofs provided by the holder.

A successful ZKP protocol must consider a number of criteria, such as scalability, interactivity, security and threat modeling, transparency, and quantum security. In order for a ZKP protocol to work effectively, it must provide sufficient privacy measures to all parties. For instance, holder and issuer should be able to maintain their anonymity while the confidentiality and untraceability of claims are still satisfied.

There is a growing interest in ZKP and the its use cases are growing. For instance, use cases around the proof of a customer's age at an establishment that serves alcoholic beverages, privacy preserving voting and membership systems, and use cases around satisfying Know Your Customer (KYC) and Anti-Money Laundering (AML) requirements while maintaining client's privacy are actively discussed within the ZKP communities. Modern SSI deployments frequently rely on CamenischLysyanskaya signatures[128], BBS+ signatures [138], and anonymous credential systems such as AnonCreds [32], which support unlinkable selective disclosure proofs compatible with W3C Verifiable Credentials.

Many organizations [139], [140] are actively working on extending ZKP protocols. Many technical groups such as ZKProof [141] aim to advance the use of ZKP by creating formal frameworks and standards around the scheme, and by promoting stronger community collaboration among different stakeholders including the academia.

Data minimization practices limit the amount of data shared to the minimum necessary to successfully accomplish a goal. Other approaches to preserving privacy recommended by W3C include selective disclosure and progressive trust. Selective disclosure is the ability for a user to have granular control over what information they share. Progressive trust is the ability for a user to gradually increase the amount of necessary data revealed as the trust is build or value generated [142].

While not covered in detail in this chapter but discussed in the privacy and SSI spaces, other notable cryptographic protocols include Homomorphic Cryptography [143], Differential Privacy [144], Identity-Based Encryption[145] and Commitment Schemes [146] which may supplement a digital identity or data management systems. Bernable et al. [147] provide a comprehensive survey of privacy-preserving research solutions within the context of blockchain and Self-Sovereign Identity systems.

In the following section, we describe the noteworthy platforms, technical groups, and organizations that are driving SSI protocols forward.

2.6 Platforms, Technical Groups, and Technology Leaders in SSI

There is a rapidly growing number of SSI platforms, industry players and technical groups committed to developing and improving the SSI and decentralized identity framework.

2.6.1 Platforms

Stacks, formerly known as Blockstack [148] is an open-source decentralized naming and storage platform built on the blockchain technology. Similar to Ethereum, Stacks supports decentralized applications; however, the computations of these applications are performed off-chain. Civic [149] is an Ethereum based decentralized identity management platform supporting a built-in incentive program. Similar to many other platforms, Civic's users use a mobile application to manage their identity data. The mobile applications are not yet open-source. uPort (now known as Serto) [150] is an SSI framework based on the Ethereum public blockchain and Interplanetary File System (IPFS) [74].

Veres One [75] is a non-profit identity project with the goal of addressing a range of existing identity challenges. Veres One supports a public permissionless network that relies on a blockchain system optimized for identity use cases. It uses verifiable credentials, decentralized key management, and DIDs to facilitate a decentralized identity management model. Similar to a number of other frameworks, Veres One relies on a board of governors – a selection of qualified members responsible for the governance of the network. Important entities include nodes that are in charge of computation and storage of the network, maintainers who are responsible for maintaining the Veres One software, and entities such as people and organizations which interact with the network to create and manage their DIDs. There is also a special role of the accelerator, responsible for increasing the speed of creation and management of DIDs.

The Hyperledger Consortium [151] is an umbrella project managed by the Linux Foundation. The objective of the Hyperledger project is to create, foster, maintain, and support open-source distributed ledger framework related projects. Hyperledger houses many DLT projects including Hyperledger Fabric [93], a general purpose DLT framework. Hyperledger also manages various DLT tools to support the development of decentralized solutions. These tools include Hyperledger Explorer and Hyperledger Composer. Currently known as one of the most popular permissioned blockchains, Hyperledger Fabric is a general purpose blockchain implementation originally developed by IBM. Fabric is developed with Golang programming language and supports pluggable consensus component, and smart-contracts (known as Chaincode), and privacy and confidentiality features required for enterprise and commercial use cases. Other notable projects within Hyperledger include Aries and Ursa. Hyperledger Aries is a blockchain-agnostic, off-ledger key and secret management system. It provides implementations of agents and ZKP-capable verifiable credentials and decentralized key management system. Hyperledger Ursa is a cryptographic library shared among many Hyperledger projects with the purpose of offering a secure, consistent and easy to use cryptographic protocols and services.

Originally developed by Evernym [139], Hyperledger Indy [94] is a public permissioned DLT solution purpose-built for decentralized identity use cases. Built from the ground up using Python and Rust programming languages, with the goal of addressing SSI use cases, Indy supports decentralized identifiers, verifiable credentials, and Zero Knowledge Proofs, while adhering to Privacy by Design principles. As oppose to storing blocks, or smart contracts, as is the case with many DLT frameworks, Indy supports the storage of DIDs and DDOs and various public identity related records such as public claims, revocation material, and consent records. No personal information is recorded on the ledger without the approval of the identity owner.

The Sovrin Network [99] is an open-source user-centric SSI framework. Sovrin is originally developed by Evernym and is managed by the Sovrin Foundation, a global non-profit organization[152]. Based on the Hyperledger Indy, the Sovrin tech stack supports

Verifiable Credentials, DIDs, agents, and Zero knowledge Proof protocols. The Sovrin distributed ledger is governed by trust anchors. Nodes in the Sovrin framework are run by stewards. There are two types of nodes, namely validator nodes, and read-only observer nodes. Sovrin stewards include companies from many continents and well-known market players such as IBM and Cisco. Sovrin supports a native protocol token to produce incentives and simplify various types of identity transactions among issuers, verifiers, and holders. The Sovrin Trust Framework [152] addresses the governance and policy aspect of the Sovrin network. It describes the processes and policies required to participate in the network, in addition to introducing various roles including trustee, trust anchor, and stewards.

Jolocom [153] is another open-source SSI platform that uses Ethereum by default that is now considered as legacy. It relies on DIDs, and hierarchical deterministic (HD) keys to generate multiple identities from a seed master identity. Every DID generated on Jolocom resolves to a DDO stored on IPFS. The mapping of every DID to DDO is performed on the Ethereum blockchain. While Jolocom SDK interfaces with Ethereum (through ERC-725 standard), the protocol is open for other blockchain implementations. Similar to other platforms, Jolocom users utilize a mobile app to interact, create, manage, and share their data.

SelfKey [154] is another SSI network where personal data is closely controlled by the users. By relying on Zero Knowledge Proofs the platform ensures only the minimum necessary amount of data is shared.

LifeID [155] is built on an open and permissionless blockchain technology and is considered as another legacy platform. It utilizes DID to generate identifiers and allow its users to control their identity data. Furthermore, LifeID relies on ZKP to ensure data minimization. A user's identity data can be backed up on cold storage, or stored with other users, or a trusted organization. LifeID has a token named ID Token to support storage and exchange of value on the network.

Mattr [156] is another SSI platform based on verifiable credentials and DIDs. The Mattr platform supports extensible data formats and secure authentication protocols. M. Kuperberg [157] provides a survey of various emerging SSI implementations. P. Dunphy et al. [158] and Andreas Abraham [159] provide further detailed comparison and analysis of the aforementioned platforms.

Another notable development is Microsoft's *ION* network, a decentralized identifier infrastructure built on top of the Bitcoin blockchain. ION implements the Sidetree protocol, a layer-two scaling solution designed to enable high-throughput decentralized identifier operations without requiring all data to be stored directly on the underlying blockchain [160]. Instead, batches of DID operations are anchored to the Bitcoin blockchain, allowing the system to maintain decentralization and security while supporting large-scale identifier management.

Another emerging identity platform is *Polygon ID*, a decentralized identity framework built on the Polygon blockchain ecosystem [161]. Similar to various other platforms, Polygon ID leverages zero-knowledge proof techniques, butit is also designed to integrate with decentralized applications and Web3 infrastructures.

Several infrastructure providers have also emerged to support the issuance and verification of verifiable credentials. *Dock Network* is a blockchain-based decentralized identity platform designed specifically to support Decentralized Identifiers and Verifiable Credentials standards [162]. Dock provides tools for credential issuance, verification, and revocation registries while supporting interoperability with existing SSI frameworks.

Similarly, *SpruceID* provides identity infrastructure focused on bridging decentralized identity systems with existing web authentication protocols [163]. The SpruceID ecosystem includes tools such as DIDKit and credential verification services that allow developers to integrate verifiable credentials into web and mobile applications while maintaining compatibility with W3C specifications.

Together, these emerging platforms illustrate the growing maturity of the SSI ecosystem. By combining decentralized identifiers, verifiable credentials, and privacy-preserving cryptographic techniques, modern SSI infrastructures aim to provide scalable, interoperable, and privacy-respecting identity management systems that can operate across institutional and national boundaries.

2.6.2 Technical Groups and Technology Leaders

The development of SSI is made possible through the work of various technical groups that help design the requirements, specification, standards, and processes for SSI.

The World Wide Web Consortium [164] is an international community that creates open standards for the web. The W3C Verifiable Credential Working Group [69] is actively working on verifiable credentials data model and use cases while the W3C Decentralized Identifier Working Group [165] is focused on developing the Decentralized Identifier specification, including its method registries and use cases. The goal of W3C Credentials Community Group [166] is to explores and draft specifications around the creation, storage, presentation and control of verifiable credentials for further standardization and prototyping.

The Rebooting of the Web of Trust (RWoT) facilitates discussions on identity related topics with a particular focus on a decentralized trust-based identity systems. The RWoT organizes annual events with the goal of producing five technical white papers on identity and trust related topics that have the biggest impact on the future of identity. Various initiatives such as DIDs, DPKI, and JSON-LD are among the initiatives examined in RWoT.

The Hyperledger Identity Group [167] promotes discussions, research and collaboration on management of digital identity data on decentralized platforms and in particular solutions related to Hyperledger.

The Internet Identity Workgroup (IIW) [168] is another technical group that meets twice a year to discuss new ideas, solutions, and initiatives with the primary focus on identity.

The Decentralized Identity Foundation (DIF) [88] is a technical organization focused on developing foundational elements required for an open ecosystem for decentralized identity. The DIF provides technical specifications and reference implementations and assists in coordinating the industry leaders. Identity Hubs and Universal Resolver are among the many projects incubated by DIF.

The Digital ID & Authentication Council (DIACC) [169] in Canada is a union of public and private sector players working together to create a trusted digital identity experience for Canadians. The Pan-Canadian Trust Framework (PCTF) spearheaded by DIACC is a framework consisting of the legal, business, and technical rules applicable to identification, authentication, and authorization, agreed on between participating public and private sector organizations across Canada.

In Europe, significant efforts are underway to build large-scale public digital identity infrastructures aligned with emerging regulatory frameworks. The European Blockchain Services Infrastructure (EBSI) is a joint initiative of the European Commission and the European Blockchain Partnership aimed at providing a pan-European distributed infrastructure for trusted digital services [170]. EBSI supports the issuance and verification of verifiable credentials across European member states and is closely aligned with the European Digital Identity Wallet introduced under the revised eIDAS 2.0 regulation.

Kantara [171] is a global non-profit organization developing specifications such as *User Managed Access* [172] and *Concept Receipt Specification*. The ID2020 [173] is a non-profit public-private consortium committed to improving lives by providing digital identity to all undocumented people worldwide. The goal of ID2020 is to provide identification for all citizens of the world by 2030. Finally, initiatives such as One World Identity (OWI) [174] and SSIMeetUP [175] provide industry practitioners the latest ideas and trends about SSI.

The OpenWallet Foundation (OWF), hosted by the Linux Foundation, focuses on developing open-source digital wallet infrastructure that supports interoperability between identity ecosystems, including verifiable credentials and decentralized identifiers [176]. The initiative aims to establish reference implementations and shared components for identity wallets that can be adopted across industries and jurisdictions.

Finally, the purpose of Trust over IP Foundation (ToIP) [177] is to provide an open and collaborative platform to define a complete architecture for Internet scale digital trust that combines both cryptographic trust at the machine layer and human trust at the business, legal, and social layers. The mission of ToIP is to combine available standards, protocols, and capabilities produced by standard development organizations and industry foundations such as W3C and DIF, to fulfill the requirements of an Internet scale digital trust architecture. The ToIP is composed of four different working groups namely Governance Stack Working Group, Technology Stack Working Group, Utility Foundry Working Group, and Ecosystem Foundry Working Group.

In the following section, we provide a summary of current and emerging privacy laws and regulations that have strongly shaped SSI and other privacy-respecting identity models.

2.7 Regulations

As privacy regulations evolve, identity systems must adapt to align with emerging legal and ethical frameworks. This section reviews major standards such as the General Data Protection Regulation (GDPR) [65], Electronic Identification, Authentication and Trust Services (eIDAS) [178], and emerging initiatives, while also proposing technical adaptations to support compliance via SSIs privacy-preserving architecture.

Data privacy regulations, in various forms, have evolved since the 16th century [179] and continue to adapt to address new technologies and expectations. Key regulations include GDPR, the Payment Service Directive (PSD3) [180], Privacy by Design (PbD) [181], and eIDAS.

The GDPR, introduced by the EU and effective since May 2018 [65], aims to harmonize data protection laws and give individuals more control over personal data. With its 11 chapters and 99 articles, it places strict requirements on consent, transparency, and data minimization. SSI aligns well with GDPR by decentralizing identity ownership and limiting unnecessary data disclosure.

Standardization efforts have also emerged to support interoperable mobile identity systems. ISO/IEC 18013-5 defines the international standard for mobile driving licences (mDL), enabling the secure storage and presentation of identity credentials on mobile devices. The standard specifies cryptographic mechanisms and communication protocols that allow digital credentials to be verified both online and offline [182].

The Payment Service Directive 2 (PSD2), effective January 2018, and it's update PSD3 enable EU consumers and businesses to authorize third-party access to financial data for innovative service delivery [180]. This mandates organizations to redesign identity and consent management frameworks. SSI offers a strong model for aligning with PSD2s emphasis on controlled consent and secure access.

eIDAS provides a regulatory foundation for trusted electronic interactions in the EU, standardizing electronic signatures, timestamps, and cross-border digital identity recognition [178]. Integrating SSI with eIDAS standards opens research opportunities for building interoperable and privacy-preserving digital identity networks. The revised Electronic Identification, Authentication and Trust Services regulation (eIDAS 2.0) introduces the European Digital Identity Wallet (EUDI Wallet), a framework that enables citizens and businesses across the European Union to store and present digital identity credentials in a secure and interoperable manner. As a result, eIDAS 2.0 represents one of the most significant regulatory developments aligning governmental identity infrastructures with concepts central to self-sovereign identity.

The National Institute of Standards and Technology (NIST) continues to refine its Digital Identity Guidelines through the SP 800-63 series, which defines technical and operational requirements for identity proofing, authentication, and federation. The most recent revision expands guidance on phishing-resistant authentication mechanisms, digital wallets, and federated identity architectures. These guidelines are widely adopted by government agencies and industry practitioners and have significantly influenced modern digital identity system design. The updated framework also recognizes emerging identity models that incorporate decentralized identity technologies and verifiable credentials [183].

Canada's Digital Charter Implementation Act introduces significant reforms to the countrys privacy and data governance framework. The legislation includes the Consumer Privacy Protection Act (CPPA), which strengthens individual rights over personal data and introduces stronger requirements for transparency, consent, and data portability. These provisions align with the broader shift toward user-centric data governance models and create a regulatory environment supportive of decentralized identity approaches. In particular, the emphasis on user control and portability of personal data reflects principles similar to those promoted by self-sovereign identity architectures [184].

Privacy by Design (PbD), developed by Ann Cavoukian in the 1990s, is a foundational framework for embedding privacy throughout system design. Its seven principles are:

a) Proactive not reactive; preventive not remedial

b) Privacy as the default setting

c) Privacy embedded into the design

d) Full functionalitypositive-sum, not zero-sum

e) End-to-end securityfull lifecycle protection

f) Visibility and transparency

g) Respect for user privacyuser-centric

These principles are particularly relevant to SSI, which enables data minimization, user-controlled disclosure, and cryptographic guarantees from the ground up.

In the United States, several states are pursuing privacy legislation. California's Consumer Privacy Act (CCPA), effective since January 2020, grants residents rights over personal data access, deletion, and sharing opt-outs [185]. While not as comprehensive as

GDPR, it reflects growing demand for user-centric privacy protections. More recently CCPA has been replaced by California Consumer Privacy Rights Act (CPRA).

Canadas Pan-Canadian Trust Framework (PCTF) is another effort to build a unified digital identity ecosystem grounded in user control, standards, and interoperability. It shares many core values with SSI.

Switzerland is also developing a government-managed digital identity system slated for launch by 2026. This model incorporates SSI concepts and decentralized data storage, with a focus on privacy protection [186].

A major development in Europe is eIDAS 2.0, which introduces the European Digital Identity Wallet (EUDI Wallet) [187]. This wallet allows EU citizens to securely store and manage credentials such as IDs and licenses. It emphasizes cross-border interoperability and aligns strongly with SSI principles like user control and data minimization.

Recent academic work further emphasizes regulatory alignment. Naghmouchi and Laurent propose a component-based analysis framework to assess how SSI implementations uphold privacy-by-design principles [188]. Their model aids developers in evaluating privacy trade-offs across the architectural layers of SSI systems.

Shehu conducts a critical review of SSI frameworks in the context of GDPR, highlighting challenges around consent enforcement, right to erasure, and data minimization [189]. The paper calls for tighter architectural and legal integration to ensure compliance under real-world conditions.

In summary, regulatory trends across regions increasingly favor decentralized, privacy-preserving identity systems. SSIs architecture offers promising alignment with this objective.

2.8 Related Research Studies

Although numerous surveys and implementations of SSI have emerged, major gaps remain in scalability, user experience, and governance design. This section identifies these limitations and synthesizes previous work to lay the groundwork for the contributions of this dissertation. Our research builds on this foundation to introduce novel identity models and design patterns that close key gaps in key management, privacy engineering, and trust negotiation.

2.8.1 Surveys

This subsection reviews key survey papers that have examined various aspects of SSI and its underlying technologies. To highlight the evolution of thought and research priorities over time, the papers are presented in chronological order.

Soltani et al. [190] provide a comprehensive survey of digital identity and its various models, including self-sovereign identity. The work further examines the core building blocks, components, and frameworks of SSI, and presents an extensive discussion of the challenges associated with this identity paradigm.

Jacobovitz [191] provides a survey of blockchain and IAM startups, foundations, and initiatives but misses various key players such as Sovrin or Hyperledger Indy. Further, the paper does not describe the purpose and goal of SSI or its building blocks.

Yang et al. [192] provide a summary of privacy preserving technologies for blockchain. These technologies include ZKP, ring signatures, homomorphic cryptography, and other cryptographic algorithms. This survey does not focus on SSI or its building blocks or provide any detail on existing or emerging identity management models.

Grüner et al. [193] assesses the use of blockchain technology for IAM through the use of a decision model on a selective group of IAM implementations namely uPort, Sovrin, and ShoCard. Based on their research both uPort and Sovrin are IAM models fit for blockchain, although because of Sovrin's strict trust framework, it can exhibit a more centralized model than uPort. The paper primarily focuses on defining and applying a decision model, offering limited discussion on the foundational components of SSI and its building blocks, or discussing privacy techniques.

In [194], Lim et al. provide a definition of various identity models, in addition to explaining and comparing three popular blockchain implementations. Moreover their paper states and compares several blockchain based identity management projects including Sovrin, ShoCard, and uPort. However, their work lacks an in-depth discussion on the standards and privacy aspects of the SSI ecosystem as well as its building blocks and principles.

Dunphy et al. [195] assess the feasibility of deploying decentralized identity models through various important requirements. These requirements include secure delegation of credentials, user experience, and methods of interacting with the blockchain. Their work also discusses the questions around the optional approaches to utilizing the unique qualities of blockchain such as immutability and transparency, for identity management purposes. However, their analysis falls short in offering a comprehensive overview of identity management, privacy engineering approaches, or the legal implications of decentralized identity systems.

In [4] Mhle et al. provide an explanation of the SSI architecture and the essential components of SSI such as verifiable credentials. Further, their work discusses the concept of identification and authentication in the context of SSI. However, their work does not discuss common SSI implementations and identity management models in detail, nor provides references to existing or emerging privacy engineering protocols.

In [157] Kuperberg provides a summary of the SSI model from the enterprise and ecosystem perspective, and compares and contrasts various SSI implementations using 75 evaluation criteria. Their work analyzes existing implementation based on system maturity and the capabilities required to compete with conventional blockchain-less solutions. While their work provides a good summary of SSI, it misses a detailed explanation of the SSI history, principles, and building blocks, in addition to any discussion around privacy engineering techniques.

NIST has published a taxonomic survey of blockchain based identity management systems [196]. Their work focuses on the terminology, model definition, and building blocks of SSI technology in addition to its privacy and security considerations. Their work, while thorough, is geared more toward the operational requirements rather than research efforts.

Tan et al. examine the shift from centralized digital identity systems toward self-sovereign identity models [197]. Their survey highlights how existing digitized identity frameworks exacerbate privacy risks and user dependency, emphasizing the growing need for decentralized architectures. The authors provide a comparative analysis of traditional identity infrastructures versus blockchain-enabled alternatives, focusing on interoperability, governance, and legal frameworks. They also explore the role of emerging standards such as decentralized identifiers and verifiable credentials in shaping the next generation of digital sovereignty.

In [198] Krul et al. present a systematization of knowledge focused on the trust relationships inherent in SSI ecosystems. The authors categorize trust assumptions across credential issuance, verification, and storage processes, identifying three core trust models: direct trust, mediated trust, and delegated trust. They systematically assess the security threats associated with each model, including metadata leakage and key compromise, and propose future research directions aimed at strengthening trust mechanisms, particularly in decentralized credential revocation and governance structures.

Chan et al. review the application of blockchain-based architectures to educational identity management, analyzing how SSI principles can address existing challenges in credential verification and student data portability [199]. The study surveys major initiatives such as Blockcerts and Open Badges 2.0, comparing their technical frameworks and governance models. It further discusses critical barriers to adoption, including credential interoperability, transaction scalability, and privacy concerns in blockchain storage of academic records. However, the survey focuses primarily on educational use cases and does not generalize its findings to broader SSI system designs or governance across different sectors.

In the article [200] by Bochnia et al., the authors investigate the role of digital wallets as critical enablers of SSI ecosystems, with a particular focus on European digital identity regulations. Their study analyzes the architecture and functionalities required for wallets to manage credentials securely, enable selective disclosure, and support user consent protocols. The authors also examine interoperability challenges between wallet providers and propose standards-based approaches to facilitate cross-jurisdictional SSI adoption under frameworks such as eIDAS 2.0.

Laatikainen et al. explore the factors influencing organizational and societal adoption of SSI technologies through empirical analysis [201]. Drawing from interviews and surveys, the study identifies technological readiness, regulatory environment, and perceived privacy benefits as key antecedents to adoption. It further outlines the expected outcomes of successful SSI deployment, including enhanced user autonomy, reduced identity verification costs, and improved interoperability across service providers. However, the work does not critically evaluate technical interoperability barriers or scalability issues, which are key technical risks affecting actual deployment of SSI systems.

Sirna provides a longitudinal analysis of the development and adoption trajectories of self-sovereign identity systems [202]. The article synthesizes findings from early pilots, such as the European Blockchain Services Infrastructure and Canada's VON initiative, to identify persistent challenges including legal fragmentation, wallet usability gaps, and limited cross-border interoperability. Sirna anticipates that future progress will hinge on the convergence of AI-driven credential management, stronger privacy-preserving techniques, and globally harmonized regulatory frameworks.

In comparison to the above surveys, this chapter fills in the missing gaps in the previous works. It provides a comprehensive overview of the digital identity and SSI, including its technical, architectural, and legal aspects as well as popular privacy engineering protocols that supplement SSI, and recent research advances in the field. As such, this chapter complements and enhances the reviews in previously published surveys.

2.8.2 Original Research and Proposals

This subsection provides an overview of SSI-based research publications, projects, and prototypes. To improve readability and thematic coherence, the following works are grouped into categories: foundational studies, domain-specific applications (e.g., healthcare and finance), privacy-enhancing techniques, legal compliance, architectural frameworks, real-world implementations, and emerging research directions such as NFTs and the Metaverse.

Foundational and Comparative Studies

Wang and De Filippi provide a description of the building blocks of SSI and discuss the Kiva case study which relies on DID, VC, and Hyperledger Indy [10]. The initial purpose of the Kiva protocol is to address the problems facing the micro-lending industry, whereby many constituents are ineligible for loans due to lack of formal identity and history. In their paper, they describe the importance of flexibility in any identity model to support the malleable nature of the human identity.

Liu et al. [203] compare traditional identity management systems with decentralized identity systems. Their assessment finds the differences stemming from their trust model and data storage schemes. They further identify maintaining privacy requirements and implementation of certain identity operations such as deletion, to be more difficult in a decentralized Identity system.

Healthcare Use Cases

Shuaib et al. propose the use of SSI in the healthcare space and provide a brief summary of available scholarly work related to the healthcare use case [204]. In addition, they state the high-level requirements of SSI adoption in healthcare and summarize the advantages of using SSI in healthcare. In paper [205], Shuhaib et al. discuss the use of the SSI model for the management of COVID-19 vaccination and test certifications.

Houtan et al. provide a survey on the use of blockchain and Self-Sovereign Identity model for management of electric patient and health records [206]. The authors provide a classification of existing frameworks, proof of concepts and published research work.

Similarly, in the health sector, patients' information is fragmented and out of the control of the patients. Various projects including MintHealth [207] have paved the way for infusing the SSI model into the current health care digital identity and trust frameworks. X. Liang et al. propose a mobile healthcare application that relies on a Hyperledger Fabric registering the hash of medical data, and cloud providers for secure storage of medical data where users have wide-ranging control over the management of their personal data [208].

Financial Services and KYC

Soltani et al. [209] developed a financial client onboarding prototype using Hyperledger Indy to demonstrate the potential of SSI in streamlining client registration. This framework is evaluated against SSI and Privacy by Design principles, as well as relevant GDPR clauses concerning personal data management.

Alex Biryukov et al. proposed a privacy preserving KYC scheme called KYCE based on the Ethereum blockchain [210]. The KYCE scheme allows users to take advantage of a unified identity to gain access to multiple financial services while preserving the privacy of the users by storing sensitive personal information with the KYC provider. Their work relies on ZKP cryptographic accumulator based on Camenisch et al. [211].

Parra-Moyano and Ross developed a KYC process based on DLT, in which a regulator maintains the database of users' personal information [212]. Upon the first interaction between a user and a bank, the user's information is shared with and verified by the bank, and upon approval, the bank places the hash representation of the user's data in blockchain. Subsequent banks rely on the hash of the data to review and confirm the authenticity of the user's data.

KYCStart [213], KYC-Chain [214] and Cambridge Blockchain [215] are among the many projects that rely on DLT to deliver streamlined and privacy-preserving KYC schemes.

Ou et al. introduce a Customer SSI (CSSI) model that allows clients to store and manage personal credit data using blockchain [216]. Financial institutions can access this data with user consent to support lending decisions. While the proposal enhances transparency and access control, the paper lacks a discussion on compliance with financial regulations.

Education and Academic Credentials

G. Dima et al. introduce the Scholarium platform [217] in which they rely on the MultiChain, a permissioned blockchain technology, to allow educational institutes to issue digital identity claims, such as graduation titles, to students. The Blockcert project [218], originally developed by the MIT Media Lab, is another pioneering blockchain-based solution for academic solutions.

Hsieh et al. present an SSI-based system for managing student portfolios in Taiwan [219]. The system uses a decentralized identity chain and a smart contract-based application chain to control how credentials are shared. Although promising, the model is currently limited to one national context and may require adaptation for broader use.

Privacy Engineering and Cryptographic Techniques

Fedrecheski et al. describe the benefits and challenges of using DIDs and VCs to identify and authenticate Internet of Things (IoT) devices and their users [220]. The authors state the main challenges to be using constrained devices to perform asymmetric cryptography, heavy communication and DID resolution, and the privacy concerns around global tracking of devices, and finally lack of options in lightweight SSI software for IoT devices.

Belchior et al. propose an SSI based access control (SSIBAC) to address the authorization and access control requirements of SSI [221]. Their proposed model relies on attribute-based model as well as selective disclosure of attributes, and range proofs for numerical values to ensure only the necessary data is disclosed to the authorized entities.

In the paper [222], the authors present B-Box, a privacy-preserving distributed storage system based on the InterPlanetary File System (IPFS) [223] and the Ethereum blockchain.

In this system, the documents are encrypted using Multi-Authority ABE, and the hash of documents returned by IPFS is stored on the Ethereum blockchain.

Axin Wu et al. [224] propose a privacy-respecting data sharing scheme based on CP-ABE and blockchain, capable of hiding the access control structure by using the attribute bloom filter.

Nabeil Eltayieb et al. [225] proposed a blockchain-based attribute-based encryption scheme for the cloud environment. In their scheme, the user's private keys are specified by a set of attributes. The encrypting party can specify a policy over these attributes to determine which users are able to decrypt the data. In the initial ABE access scheme proposed in [226], the ciphertext and the user's key are associated with a set of attributes. In addition, a threshold value k is added to the user's key. A user is able to decrypt a ciphertext as long as there is at least k attributes overlapped between the attributes in the private key and the ciphertext. However, this form of threshold semantics is not very expressive and limits the design of more generic models.

The term 'data capsule' has been used in different contexts and for different applications, including privacy-preserving data models [227][228][229]. In paper [227], the authors describe a container of a subject's data along with its access policy governing how the data is processed. The authors introduce a formal privacy policy language capable of encoding data privacy requirements. In paper [228], the authors propose a model to encapsulate sensitive personal data along with policies that support fine-grained access control, with support for data transformation before the data is shared with service providers to ensure data minimization. In paper [229], the authors define the data capsule as a generic representational specification of data for a cloud-edge computational architecture for autonomous robots.

Mukta et al. [230] propose CredChain, a SSI system that enables the creation, sharing, and verification of credentials, in addition to flexible and selective disclosure of claims using redactable signatures [231].

Dieye et al. propose a novel SSI protocol that uses two ZKP schemes based on discrete logarithms, allowing a user to prove identity attributes without revealing sensitive information [232]. The protocol uses automorphism groups to link multiple claims under one identity. While the scheme is mathematically sound, the authors provide no implementation or benchmark testing.

Regulatory and Legal Compliance

In paper [233], Naik and Jenkins evaluate the compatibility of uPort and Sovrin SSI ecosystem against GDPR principles, with the conclusion that those SSI systems are based on public permissioned blockchain are able to comply with the majority of key GDPR principles.

G. Kondova and J. Erbguth provide an assessment of Sovrin, uPort, and Jolocom SSI platforms, and analyze the arising issues related to GDPR and SSI [234]. Their paper raises various privacy concerns around SSI, and focus on the issues around the storage of four types of data namely DIDs, verifiable credentials, revocation data, and cryptographically hashed data.

Architectures and Integration Frameworks

Asem Othman and John Callahan propose the Horcrux protocol [235], a decentralized authentication model, in which they rely on decentralized identifiers and IEEE 2410-2017 Biometric Open Protocol Standard (BOPS) to develop an SSI solution capable of storing decentralized biometric credentials.

M. Takemiya et al. propose the Sora SSI Identity Protocol [236]. This protocol relies on Hyperledger Iroha and DIDs and utilizes a central server to store encrypted copies of users' cryptographic keys and personal data. The Sora protocol supports the storage of salted hash representation of the users' identity data, along with the associated digital signatures generated by the identity issuers, on to the blockchain. This feature provides support for identity validation, non-repudiation, and time-locking capabilities.

In [237], Zoltan Lux et al. provide a proof-of-concept integration of SSI and OpenID

Connect protocol on Hyperledger Indy, with ability for the users to choose from a pool of identity providers instead of a select few. Their proposed system is able to receive OIDC claims as Verifiable Credentials.

M. Schanzenbach et al. developed reclaimID, an SSI platform for the peer-to-peer exchange of claim by utilizing the GNU Name System (GNS) [238]. The GNS system relies on a distributed hash table (DHT) and supports encrypted records, queries, and responses. The attributes stored on the name system are managed using attribute-based encryption allowing users to selectively disclose required attributes with the requesting parties.

Finally, A. Abraham et al. propose a proof of concept to realize the derivation of digital identity attributes issued by traditional identity management systems into an SSI system based on Hyperledger Indy [239]. Their work also extends Hyperledger Indy's consensus protocol to support additional features including multi-signature operations and verification of signatures contained in identity assertions.

Government and Institutional Deployments

Governments around the world are exploring the potential of SSI. The Canadian province of British Columbia has developed a platform called Verified Organization Network (VON) based on Hyperledger Indy, to allow organizations to manage their verified claims [240]. Likewise, The USs Department of Homeland Securitys Science and Technology Directorate has invested in the development of SSI standards [241]. Estonia's e-residency system provides applicants outside of Estonia the possibility to register a company or open a bank account [242]. Finally, Australias post office and Digital Transformation Office have explored blockchain-based identity management systems [243].

Emerging Research: NFTs and the Metaverse

Wajiha Rehman et al. provide a summary of NFT, major challenges, NFT marketplaces and, NFT use cases and applications [244]. They further provide a breakdown of the NFT challenges to cover intellectual property rights, security, privacy, flaws in smart contract code, and environmental impacts. They indicate copyright theft and fraud as one of the major security challenges.

Andrew Park et al. [245] provide a taxonomy of use cases for NFT covering current and future applications and highlighting the challenges in integrating NFTs in existing workflows.

S. Casale-Brunet et al. [246] give an overview of the most common NFT collection and provide a topological structure and analysis of NFT networks covering major NFT projects such as CryptoPunks, and discussing the patterns identified through analyzing the wallets participating in this ecosystem.

2.9 Conclusion

In this chapter, we examined the fundamental concepts of identity, digital identity, and identity and access management, tracing their evolution through successive architectural models culminating in Self-Sovereign Identity. We analyzed the structural limitations of traditional identity management approaches, highlighting the security, privacy, and user autonomy challenges inherent in centralized and federated identity systems. The chapter further introduced the technological foundations that enable decentralized identity architectures, including decentralized identifiers, verifiable credentials, decentralized public key infrastructures, and privacy-preserving cryptographic protocols.

Our analysis demonstrates that although existing identity management frameworks have improved digital service access and authentication capabilities, they remain fundamentally dependent on centralized intermediaries and third-party control. Self-Sovereign Identity represents a significant paradigm shift by enabling individuals to manage and present their identity attributes through decentralized trust mechanisms while preserving privacy and minimizing unnecessary data disclosure.

Beyond establishing the conceptual and technical foundations of decentralized identity, this chapter provides the necessary context for the research contributions developed in the subsequent chapters. The architectural principles, cryptographic mechanisms, and governance considerations introduced here motivate the novel identity management architectures and algorithms proposed in this dissertation, which aim to address outstanding challenges in identity portability, consent management, and resilient cryptographic identity infrastructures.

Chapter 3

Key Management and Recovery

This chapter introduces a novel approach to decentralized key management tailored for SSI digital wallets. The proposed model addresses the pressing need for secure, usable, and privacy-preserving key recovery mechanisms that can operate without reliance on centralized authorities.

3.1 Introduction

Existing identity management models heavily rely on centralized repositories for storing identity data and cryptographic keys. This reliance has led to a rising number of security breaches, data loss incidents, and significant costs for all stakeholders, particularly identity owners.

The SSI model offers a more user-centric approach to identity management, where users take control of their secret keys and identity information through digital wallets. However, while the SSI model addresses some of the limitations of centralized systems, it also introduces several unique challenges that must be resolved for widespread adoption.

A significant challenge lies in the design of secure, practical, and privacy-preserving approaches to key management. Unlike traditional identity management systems, which rely on trusted third parties for key management, the SSI model places the responsibility squarely on identity owners. Without proper protocols in place, this shift can lead to vulnerabilities, data loss, and fraud, undermining the promise of SSI.

Digital wallets are a critical component of the SSI ecosystem, enabling users to manage secret keys, identity claims, and other personal information. Effective and privacy-preserving key management protocols are essential for the adoption of digital wallets, particularly in contexts such as SSI and cryptocurrency.

In this chapter, we propose a practical key backup and recovery protocol based on threshold secret-sharing cryptography. The protocol leverages multiple third-party key escrow providers, each of whom holds a share of the user's secret key. The secret key can only be reconstructed when a predefined minimum number of participants collaborate. Additionally, the execution of this protocol, including parameters such as the minimum number of participants required and the role of the user, is fully configurable within the proposed digital wallet application. The remainder of this chapter presents the foundational building blocks, the proposed recovery architecture, implementation details, security analysis, and experimental evaluation.

3.2 Building Blocks

The proposed system architecture is built upon three foundational components that collectively enable secure, decentralized identity management and robust support for the cryptographic key life cycle. These components are as follows:

- Digital wallets, which securely store and manage identity credentials and cryptographic keys.
- A decentralized key management system, which ensures distributed control, integrity, and resilience of key-related operations.
- Key backup and recovery mechanisms, designed to preserve user access in the event of device loss, compromise, or failure.

This section provides a detailed examination of each building block and explains how they interact to support practical and deployable self-sovereign identity systems.

3.2.1 Digital Wallets

Physical wallets have long been a fundamental tool for carrying personal items, evolving significantly over time. A wallet traditionally holds items such as financial cards, ID cards, cash, receipts, business cards, photographs, and coupons.

As discussed in Chapter 2, a digital wallet replicates nearly all the functions of a traditional wallet in a digital format. As a software component running on a smartphone, serving as an electronic equivalent of a physical wallet, a digital wallet can store various types of information, including payment details, coupons, and, in some cases, identity credentials.

In the context of the SSI model, a digital wallet stores diverse identity-related information, such as key pairs, credentials, tokens, and optionally, service endpoints. Furthermore, a digital wallet can establish secure communication with other entities to facilitate authentication or exchange of information.

3.2.2 Decentralized Key Management System

The Decentralized Key Management System (DKMS) is an emerging open standard for managing cryptographic keys in a decentralized architecture, ensuring that no single party can compromise the overall integrity and security of the system [247]. DKMS wallets are designed to work seamlessly with decentralized systems, such as distributed ledger technology and blockchain, without relying on a central authority. DKMS therefore provides a natural foundation for decentralized key backup and recovery mechanisms in SSI wallets.

3.2.3 Common Key Backup and Recovery Methods

The storage and recovery of cryptographic keys are critical components of decentralized key management systems. Various approaches have been proposed and studied in both academia and industry. This section outlines a selection of common methods in greater detail.

Secure Elements and Trusted Execution Environment

Secure Elements (SE) integrate hardware, software, and protocols within devices to enable the secure storage of sensitive information. A Trusted Execution Environment (TEE) is an isolated and protected processing environment, separate from the main processing environment [248].

A TEE includes processing, storage, and memory capabilities that remain secure, even if the main operating system is compromised. As mentioned previously, popular implementations of TEE include ARM TrustZone and Intel SGX. Similarly, hardware security modules (HSMs) are specialized hardware components designed to securely store private keys and perform cryptographic operations [249].

Biometrics

First proposed by Bodo [250], biometric-based key management has been extensively researched [251]. Biometric traits are portable and, to a significant degree, unique, making them suitable as seed values for generating cryptographic keys.

Secure Cloud Storage and Key Escrows

Another common approach to key backup and recovery involves storing secret keys with trusted third-party repositories, also known as key escrow providers. Secure cloud-based storage services can be offered by entities in both the public and private sectors, such as financial institutions, telecommunication providers, and government agencies.

Mnemonics and QR Code Technology

To aid in the memorization of secret keys, mnemonic wordsoften referred to as seed phrasescan be derived from cryptographic keys. Additionally, secret keys can be represented as QR codes, providing a convenient and portable method for storage and retrieval.

3.3 The Proposed Model

In this section, we present our decentralized key backup and recovery model, which is based on Shamir's threshold secret-sharing algorithm. In this model, the user possesses a digital wallet capable of generating cryptographic secret keys and performing secure backup and restoration of those keys.

Building blocks to support the proposed model

Privacy is defined as the limitation of the information exposed by the distributed computation to only the information that can be learned from the designated output of the computation [118]. Secure Multi-Party Computation (SMC) [252] provides a privacy-preserving method for a group of entities to jointly compute a function over their inputs without sharing these inputs with other parties or relying on a trusted third party. The SMC is a well-studied problem in cryptography.

For instance, consider three parties: Alice, Charlie, and Bobwith secret inputs x, y, and z representing their respective salaries. To find the highest salary among them without revealing their salaries to one another, they can engage in an SMC protocol. The output of the protocol is the highest salary, which can then be compared by each party. Mathematically, this is expressed as $F(x, y, z) = max(x, y, z)$.

As described in Chapter 2, Shamir's secret sharing algorithm can be described as follows: A user V splits a secret K into n shares, such that any combination of $< t$ shares cannot learn the secret K , while any combination of $\geq t$ shares can learn the secret K.

Throughout this chapter, we denote the master secret key as K and individual shares generated via Shamirs Secret Sharing as K_i. Moreover, let n denote the total number of registered escrow providers, and let tn denote the recovery threshold. During recovery, the wallet may contact any subset of size mt.

3.3.1 Architecture

We model a digital wallet capable of securely storing sensitive information, such as cryptographic keys and identity credentials, within the secure element of a mobile device. The digital wallet can perform backup and recovery of secret keys using a distributed and privacy-preserving approach. By leveraging the threshold secret-sharing algorithm, the digital wallet splits the user's cryptographic keys into multiple shares and distributes them to carefully selected third parties, referred to as key escrow providers.

In our model, the digital wallet is the only entity with access to the user's complete secret keys. The key escrow providers run a specialized digital wallet implementation that can engage in key exchange protocols with the user's digital wallet.

The key escrow service can be offered by various trusted entities, such as telecommunication providers, banks, or credit unions. To enhance neutrality and trustworthiness, the system combines multiple key escrow providers. Furthermore, utilizing providers with opposing interests is an approach we consider to further strengthen the trust model.

Our architecture supports three core operations: key generation and registration, key backup, and key recovery.

A) Secret Key Generation and Registration

The first step of key management describes the method by which a user generates a cryptographic key pair. The cipher suite used to generate the keys depends on the hardware capabilities of the mobile device, the capabilities of the digital wallet, user's preference and the purpose of the keys. The digital wallet is capable of storing the generated secret keys within the mobile device's secure element. During the registration phase, the digital wallet performs a scan of the network to seek available key escrow providers and allow the user to register them as possible options for the key backup and recovery procedures.

B) Secret Key Backup Process

After successfully generating secret keys, the digital wallet enables the user to create backups of any cryptographic key. Given a cryptographic key K and set of n escrow providers $P = \{p_1, \ldots, p_n\}$, the digital wallet splits the key into a set of shares $\{K_1, \ldots, K_n\}$ for n participants. The user specifies the threshold value t, which represents the minimum number of participants required to reconstruct the secret. This threshold is determined based on the user's preferences and the availability of key escrow providers. Each bundle is encrypted as $M_i = E(PubK_i, \{K_i, B_i\})$, where $PubK_i$ is the public key of the key escrow provider i. Finally, the wallet securely transmits the encrypted payload M_i to the respective escrow provider i.

C) Secret Key Recovery Process

To recover the secret key K, the digital wallet attempts to establish a secure communication channel with key escrow providers from the set P until it retrieves shares from at least t distinct providers. Once at least t key shares are retrieved, the wallet uses the key shares and Lagrange interpolation to reconstruct the polynomial function $f(x)$ defined during setup. Finally, by evaluating $f(0)$, the wallet is able to recover the original secret key K. The secret is then stored within the device's secure element.

3.3.2 Implementation

To implement the proposed model, we developed a Python-based prototype that captures the core backup and recovery workflows described in this chapter. While the prototype executes the cryptographic operations and provider interactions using lightweight REST services, the design is informed by Hyperledger Indys SSI architecture. In a production deployment, Hyperledger Indy can provide the decentralized identity layer to support DID and DID Documents for publishing and resolving public keys and service endpoints so that the Indy ledger acts as the root of trust for discovering and authenticating key escrow

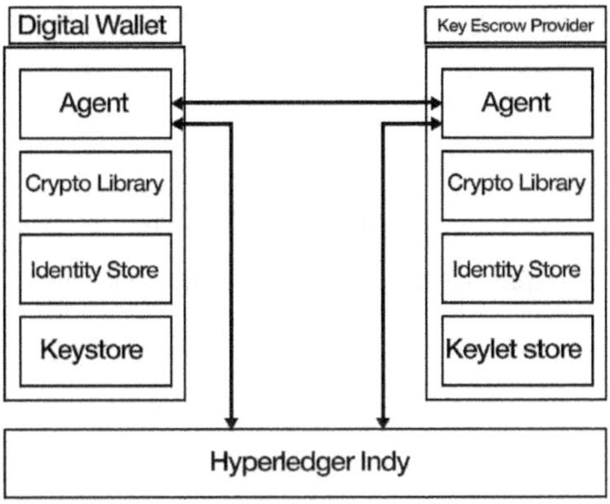

Figure 3.1: High-level architecture of the decentralized key backup and recovery model

providers and establishing secure wallet-to-provider interactions. Figure 3.1 depicts the high-level architecture of our model.

The digital wallet application is designed for this work with the following components:

- **Agent:** Responsible for establishing secure communication channels with other agents using the DID communication protocol. The agent also handles key backup and recovery requests.
- **Cryptographic Libraries:** Implements key management functionalities, including Shamir's secret-sharing algorithm for secure key backup and recovery.
- **Identity Store:** Maintains user identity data, such as DIDs and associated metadata, within a secure enclave.
- **Key Store:** Stores secret keys generated, supporting multiple cryptographic algorithms.

3.3.3 Security Parameters

To evaluate the proposed key backup and recovery model, a prototype was implemented in Python using the `cryptography` library for secure key operations. The secret sharing scheme employs Shamir's threshold secret sharing over the Galois field defined by the 521-bit Mersenne prime

$$P = 2^{521} - 1 \tag{3.1}$$

which provides sufficient capacity for 256-bit secret keys while maintaining computational efficiency. The implementation generates cryptographically secure random secret K of 32 bytes (256 bits) using Python's `secrets` module and constructs a random polynomial of degree $(t - 1)$ with the secret as the constant term, where t represents the threshold parameter. Each share consists of a unique x-coordinate (sequential integers 1 to n) and the corresponding y-value computed by evaluating the polynomial. The biometric binding mechanism utilizes SHA-256 to compute provider-specific identifiers as

$$B_i = \text{SHA256}(\text{PubKey}_i \| B) \tag{3.2}$$

where PubKey_i is the RSA public key of escrow provider i and B is the user's biometric template. For asymmetric encryption between the wallet and escrow providers, RSA-OAEP with 4096-bit keys, SHA-256 as both the OAEP hash and MGF1 hash, and public exponent 65537 is employed. The communication protocol uses RESTful HTTP endpoints with Base64-encoded JSON payloads, where backup requests contain the encrypted tuple $\{K_i, B_i\}$ and recovery requests contain the encrypted biometric identifier B_i. The implementation supports configurable threshold parameters (t-of-n schemes) with the constraint $1 \leq t \leq n$, allowing users to select the appropriate security-availability tradeoff for their use case.

The digital wallet follows **a two-step process** for key backup and recovery:

A) Secret Key Backup Process

When a user selects the key backup option, the wallet automatically initiates a backup procedure as described below:

a) The wallet requests the number of key escrow providers, denoted as n, and a threshold value t, which represents the minimum number of shares required to recover the original key.

b) The secret key K of 32 bytes is split into n shares using Shamirs Secret Sharing scheme, assigning one share K_i to each key escrow provider $i \in \{1, \ldots, n\}$.

c) The wallet captures a biometric template B from the user.

d) For each key escrow provider i, the wallet performs the following steps:

   (a) The wallet retrieves the public key $PubK_i$ of escrow provider i.

   (b) The wallet generates a unique biometric-derived hash for provider i as:

$$B_i = H(PubK_i \,\|\, B)$$

   where $H : \{0,1\}^* \to \{0,1\}^{256}$ is a cryptographic hash function SHA-256.

   (c) The wallet encrypts the tuple $\{K_i, B_i\}$ using the providers public key:

$$M_i = E(PubK_i, \{K_i, B_i\})$$

   (d) The encrypted tuple M_i is transmitted to escrow provider i.

   (e) The key escrow provider decrypts M_i using its private key and stores the result as a key-value pair: (B_i, K_i).

e) Finally, the original secret key K and biometric template B are securely deleted from device memory to minimize data leakage and exposure.

Each share is encrypted using the recipients public key, ensuring confidentiality during transmission. The wallet can securely transmit each encrypted share to a registered key escrow provider using a RESTful API over HTTPS with TLS authentication.

B) Secret Key Recovery Process

The recovery process is triggered when a user requests to restore their cryptographic key:

a) The digital wallet performs discovery for available key escrow providers. For example, the wallet can query the registry to identify registered providers by resolving their decentralized identifiers to obtain service endpoints and public keys required for secure communication.

   The wallet may prioritize providers that were previously registered during the backup phase if such information is available. Alternatively, the user may manually provide the URL or DID of known key escrow providers.

   Once a set of candidate providers is identified, the wallet establishes secure communication channels with a subset of these providers to retrieve the required key shares.

b) The wallet obtains the public key $PubK_i$ of each selected key escrow provider $i \in \{1, \ldots, m\}$.

c) The wallet captures a fresh biometric scan from the user and generates a biometric template B.

d) For each key escrow provider i, the wallet performs the following steps:

   (a) The wallet generates a unique biometric-derived hash:

   $$B_i = H(PubK_i \,\|\, B)$$

   where $H()$ is a cryptographic hash function SHA-256.

   (b) The wallet encrypts the biometric identifier:

   $$M_i = E(PubK_i, B_i)$$

(c) The encrypted message M_i is transmitted to escrow provider i.

(d) The key escrow provider decrypts M_i using its private key, and looks up the corresponding share K_i associated with B_i.

(e) The provider returns the recovered share K_i to the wallet.

e) If the wallet successfully retrieves at least t shares from distinct escrow providers, it proceeds with the reconstruction process.

f) The wallet applies Lagrange interpolation on the retrieved shares $\{K_i\}_{i \in I}$, where $|I| \geq t$, to reconstruct K.

g) The reconstructed key K is securely stored in the wallet's key store.

3.3.4 Assumptions and Discussion

In the proposed protocol, an encrypted communication channel between every digital wallet and key escrow provider is assumed. Additionally, we assume that the digital wallet can successfully authenticate the user and is the only trusted entity capable of generating, backing up, recovering, and storing the cryptographic keys. This assumption extends to the availability and semi-trustworthiness of the key escrow providers.

The proposed model defines an architecture in which no single entity other than the user's digital wallet has access to the full secret key. Furthermore, collaboration among fewer than t key escrow providers will not suffice to reconstruct the original key, preserving the threshold security property of the scheme. To enhance resilience, the user's digital wallet may also store one or more key shares locally, effectively acting as an additional key escrow provider.

As the threshold value t increases, the overall security of the system improves. However, this may negatively impact efficiency. Similarly, increasing the total number of key escrow providers n may introduce additional overhead and reduce performance.

Key recovery mechanisms must be deployed with great care. If improperly implemented, such protocols can weaken the overall security of the system. A fundamental security requirement of our model is that the effort required to compromise the system should be no less than the effort needed to break a traditional key recovery protocol based on a single trusted third party [253].

To encrypt messages to each key escrow provider, the user's wallet must have access to the corresponding public keys. This requirement can be fulfilled through a decentralized trust model based on distributed ledger technology, which allows the wallet to look up the public keys and service endpoints of key escrow providers. Finally, the model assumes that the wallet can verify the identity of each provider through the validation of their digital certificates.

Another important consideration is the consistency and uniqueness of the biometric data captured from the user. Biometric inputs, such as fingerprints or facial features, are inherently noisy and may vary slightly between captures due to environmental conditions, sensor quality, or user interaction. To ensure reliable key recovery, the system must incorporate mechanisms for stabilizing biometric representations across multiple capture instances. Techniques such as biometric fuzzy extractors [254] or fuzzy commitment schemes [255] can be employed to derive a consistent and repeatable cryptographic representation from inherently variable biometric inputs. These approaches allow the system to tolerate minor variations in biometric data while still producing a stable identifier suitable for secure key retrieval. Without such mechanisms, inconsistencies in biometric capture could lead to failed recovery attempts, negatively impacting usability and system reliability.

Lastly, to further enhance the security of the system, the architecture can be extended to incorporate biometric-based encryption of key shares prior to distribution [256]. In this enhanced model, each share K_i can be encrypted using a key derived from the users biometric data, in addition to the public-key encryption already employed for secure transmission. As a result, even if an adversary compromises a key escrow provider and gains access to stored data, the attacker would still be unable to recover the underlying share without access to the corresponding biometric-derived key. This adds an additional layer of protection against insider threats, collusion among providers, and large-scale data breaches. However, this approach introduces additional complexity in key management and requires careful handling of biometric-derived keys to avoid usability issues or irreversible data loss. Therefore, while biometric-based encryption strengthens confidentiality guarantees, it must be carefully balanced with robustness and recoverability considerations in practical deployments.

3.3.5 Security Analysis

The security of the proposed key recovery model hinges on the combination of cryptographic threshold schemes and biometric-derived binding. Below, we analyze the models robustness against key threats, using formal assumptions and security properties grounded in cryptographic theory.

Adversary Model

We assume the presence of a semi-honest adversary $\mathcal{A}$ who may compromise up to $t - 1$ key escrow providers and attempt to:

- Reconstruct the secret key without authorization.
- Spoof the user's biometric input to retrieve shares.
- Extract biometric information from stored data.

We further assume that:

- All communications between the wallet and providers are encrypted and authenticated (e.g., TLS with mutual authentication).
- Biometric hashes use a preimage-resistant hash function (e.g., SHA-256).
- The Shamirs Secret Sharing scheme is information-theoretically secure.

Formal Security Claims and Justifications

- **Threshold Confidentiality:** The scheme provides information-theoretic guarantees that fewer than t shares yield no knowledge of the original key.

  Proof Sketch: In Shamirs Secret Sharing, the secret K is the constant term of a random degree-$(t-1)$ polynomial $f(x)$ over a finite field $\mathbb{F}_p$. Given fewer than t points, the polynomial remains underdetermined, and the entropy of K remains maximal (uniform over $\mathbb{F}_p$).

- **Share Confidentiality and Biometric Binding:** Each escrow provider stores only a *single share* K_i and never observes the master secret K. During backup, the wallet transmits the encrypted payload $M_i = E(PubK_i, \{K_i, B_i\})$ so that (i) K_i is confidential in transit and (ii) only provider i can decrypt and store the share using its private key. Here, the value $B_i = H(PubK_i \parallel B)$ acts as a *provider-specific access token* derived from the users biometric material B and the provider identity (via $PubK_i$). The inclusion of $PubK_i$ ensures that the same user produces different identifiers across different providers, preventing cross-provider correlation of stored identifiers.

  During recovery, the wallet must recompute the correct B_i from a fresh biometric capture (or an equivalent stable biometric-derived secret) in order to retrieve the corresponding share K_i from provider i. Thus, biometric binding in this protocol is realized as *gated share release*: even if an adversary compromises the storage of a provider and obtains (B_i, K_i), they still require at least t shares *and* the ability to pass the biometric-based lookup step at each provider to complete recovery.

  Assumption: The hash function H is preimage-resistant and collision-resistant, and the public-key encryption scheme E is IND-CCA secure. Biometric material B is assumed to be processed into a stable representation suitable for consistent regeneration across recovery attempts.

- **Biometric Spoofing Resistance:** An adversary who learns public parameters (including $PubK_i$) still cannot retrieve a share from provider i unless they can reproduce a biometric-derived secret that yields the correct provider-specific identifier $B_i = H(PubK_i \parallel B)$. Assuming B is derived from a live biometric capture (or an equivalent stable biometric-derived secret), an attacker must either (i) successfully spoof the biometric input so that the wallet derives the same B, or (ii) guess a value that hashes to the stored B_i, which is computationally infeasible under the preimage resistance of H. Therefore, brute-force recovery of B_i is infeasible, and successful spoofing reduces to the difficulty of defeating the underlying biometric authentication mechanism.

- **Collusion Resistance:** Even if multiple escrow providers collude, any coalition of fewer than t providers learns only their local shares $\{K_i\}$ and cannot reconstruct the master secret K due to the information-theoretic security of Shamirs Secret Sharing. Moreover, colluding providers do not gain the ability to validate or regenerate the users biometric-derived secret B; they only observe provider-specific identifiers (e.g., B_i) and their associated shares. Consequently, compromising privacy or recovering K requires both meeting the threshold ($\geq t$ distinct shares) and passing the biometric-gated retrieval step at each participating provider.

- **Impersonation Considerations:** The recovery protocol binds each key share K_i to a biometric-derived identifier $B_i = H(PubK_i \parallel B)$, ensuring that only a user capable of reproducing the correct biometric-derived secret can successfully retrieve shares from escrow providers. This mechanism provides resistance against impersonation attacks in which an adversary attempts to request key shares without access to the users biometric input.

- **Leakage Resistance:** If encrypted payloads $M_i = E(PubK_i, \{K_i, B_i\})$ are intercepted or leaked, the confidentiality of the underlying share K_i is preserved under the IND-CCA security of the public-key encryption scheme. IND-CCA (Indistinguishability under Adaptive Chosen-Ciphertext Attack) guarantees that an adversary who can adaptively request decryptions of arbitrary ciphertexts excluding the target ciphertext cannot distinguish encryptions of chosen plaintexts with non-negligible advantage [257, 258].

Under this assumption, observing or storing encrypted messages does not reveal any information about K_i or B_i without access to the corresponding private key. Consequently, ciphertext leakage alone does not enable recovery of key shares nor assist in reconstructing the master secret K, unless the adversary additionally compromises at least t escrow provider private keys.

Security Reductions and Comparisons

- **Reduction to Multiple Hard Problems:** Compromising the proposed system requires an adversary to simultaneously:
  - obtain at least t valid secret shares from distinct escrow providers,
  - successfully reproduce the biometric-derived secret required to retrieve each share, and
  - compromise at least t escrow providers (e.g., by obtaining their private decryption keys) or otherwise defeat the underlying public-key encryption mechanisms.

  Failure in any one of these steps prevents reconstruction of the master secret key K.

- **Comparison with single-provider Escrow Models:** In contrast to traditional key escrow architectures that rely on a single trusted entity, the proposed model distributes trust across multiple independent providers. Assuming independent compromise probabilities, the likelihood of total system failure decreases rapidly as the threshold parameter t increases, providing substantially stronger resilience than single-provider designs.

- **Threshold Trust Decentralization:** The system enforces threshold trust decentralization, meaning that security failure occurs only if a quorum of escrow providers is compromised *and* the adversary successfully bypasses biometric authentication. This combined requirement represents a significantly higher attack barrier than conventional centralized key recovery mechanisms.

3.4 Experimental Results

To evaluate the performance and effectiveness of the proposed key recovery model, we developed a prototype implementation within a digital wallet environment. The evaluation focuses on the following key metrics:

- **Key Backup Latency:** The time required to generate a biometric-derived identifier, split the secret key using Shamir's Secret Sharing, encrypt each share, and transmit the encrypted payloads to the selected key escrow providers.

- **Key Recovery Latency:** The time required to recapture the user's biometric input, generate provider-specific biometric hashes, retrieve a sufficient number of key shares, and reconstruct the original secret key.

3.4.1 Key Backup and Recovery Latency

The prototype was deployed on a MacBook Pro equipped with an Apple M1 Pro processor running macOS Sonoma 14.5. The implementation uses simulated biometric input, secure local storage, and REST-based communication with locally emulated key escrow providers. All cryptographic operations were performed using RSA-OAEP for encryption and Shamirs Secret Sharing for key splitting and reconstruction. Requests to escrow providers were issued sequentially.

Table 3.1 reports the end-to-end latency for key backup and recovery under two representative threshold configurations. Each experiment was executed 30 times, and both average and maximum observed latencies are reported.

Operation	Average Latency (ms)	Max Latency (ms)
Key Backup (3-of-5 scheme)	34	40
Key Backup (5-of-7 scheme)	50	94
Key Recovery (3-of-5 scheme)	21	27
Key Recovery (5-of-7 scheme)	35	41

Table 3.1: End-to-end key backup and recovery latency measured with RSA-OAEP encryption and REST-based escrow providers.

The results indicate that both backup and recovery operations complete within acceptable time bounds for lightweight, interactive applications. As expected, recovery latency increases with the number of key shares involved due to additional biometric hash computations, cryptographic operations, and network requests.

To better understand the sources of latency, Table 3.2 presents an approximate per-provider breakdown of the dominant cost components. They shows where the time is spent during a single interaction with one key escrow provider. These measurements were obtained by instrumenting the prototype during execution.

Component	Average Time (ms)
RSA-OAEP encryption (wallet)	0.2
HTTP request/response (localhost REST)	6
RSA-OAEP decryption (provider)	0.2
Provider storage and lookup	0.01

Table 3.2: Per-provider latency breakdown for the escrow interaction in the prototype implementation.

This breakdown shows that the dominant contributors to latency are network communication overhead. This indicates that optimizing performance should focus on reducing communication overhead, for example through parallel requests or batching, rather than optimizing cryptographic primitives. The cost of polynomial interpolation during recovery was negligible for the tested thresholds. This is expected as interpolation has low computational complexity and does not scale significantly with small threshold values which are practical in production.

3.4.2 Threshold Scaling Analysis

The threshold parameter t determines the minimum number of escrow providers required for key reconstruction and directly influences both security and performance. Increasing t improves resilience against partial compromise but introduces additional latency, as more providers must be contacted during recovery.

Table 3.3 summarizes the average recovery latency observed for several threshold configurations. The experiments include every steps required for recovery including network, decryption and interpolation. The results demonstrate a predictable, approximately linear increase in recovery time as t increases, reflecting the sequential nature of provider communication in the current prototype.

Threshold Configuration (t-of-n)	**Average Recovery Latency (ms)**
2-of-3	14
3-of-5	20
5-of-7	34

Table 3.3: Impact of threshold value on key recovery latency when considering the total latency for decr.

Despite the linear increase in latency at higher thresholds, recovery times remain well within acceptable bounds for user-driven recovery workflows. In a production deployment, parallel requests and native cryptographic APIs would further reduce end-to-end latency.

3.5 Conclusion

This chapter introduced a novel key recovery model aimed at addressing a critical challenge in self-sovereign identity systems: how to securely and practically recover cryptographic keys without relying on a single trusted authority. While current SSI frameworks provide mechanisms for decentralized identifiers and credential issuance, they often overlook the complexity of key recovery in the event of device loss or user error.

The proposed solution integrates Shamirs threshold secret-sharing scheme with biometric-derived identifiers to enable secure, user-centric key recovery.In this model, a secret key is split into multiple shares and distributed across key escrow providers. Each share is protected using a deterministic, provider-specific biometric hash that is unique to both the user and the corresponding provider, such that successful retrieval of shares is conditioned on reproducing the correct biometric-derived secret.

This approach strengthens the overall security of the recovery process by eliminating reliance on static credentials and preventing unauthorized access to shares, even if an escrow provider is compromised. The model enforces threshold-based reconstruction, ensuring that no single provider can compromise the secret on its own.

Our prototype implementation demonstrates that the proposed approach can operate efficiently on modern devices under realistic, user-driven workflows. By combining biometric-derived access control with decentralized key escrow, this chapter presents a practical and security-conscious solution to the longstanding problem of key recovery in self-sovereign identity systems.

Chapter 4

Addressing SSI Access Control through Data Capsules

This chapter presents a novel cryptographic framework, referred to as the *Data Capsule (DC) model*, which introduces a new class of access control mechanisms tailored specifically for self-sovereign identity systems. Unlike conventional approaches that rely on service providers to evaluate and enforce access policies, the Data Capsule model shifts enforcement to the cryptographic layer, enabling self-contained and self-enforcing data objects. This solution fills an important enforcement gap in which authorization is procedural rather than cryptographically guaranteed.

Each Data Capsule securely binds encrypted personal data with an embedded access policy using attribute-based encryption, verifiable credentials, and decentralized identifiers. The model further leverages blockchain-based registries to support transparent publication and retrieval of access policy schemas, enabling independent verification of declared authorization requirements.

This framework departs from existing SSI data-sharing practices by reducing reliance on intermediary trust, limiting unnecessary exposure of personal data, and enabling recipient-specific selective disclosure. The chapter presents an end-to-end model that integrates attribute-based access control with verifiable data structures and a ledger-backed access-policy registry into a single, portable cryptographic container. The remainder of this chapter presents the motivation, architecture, and proof-of-concept implementation of the proposed model.

4.1 Introduction

With the increasing prevalence of online interactions and digital service delivery, there is growing reliance on the electronic exchange of personally identifiable information. At the same time, the continued rise in security incidents, data breaches, and unauthorized surveillance has raised significant concerns regarding the adequacy of existing identity and access management models. As discussed in Chapter 2, many of these models place service providers at the center of the ecosystem, granting them broad control over sensitive user data with limited transparency or accountability.

Although regulatory frameworks such as the GDPR and CCPA provide structured guidelines for protecting personal data, enforcement is often reactive, with violations and misuse detected only after public disclosure. Furthermore, transparency into how access decisions are enforced at a technical level remains limited [259]. We argue that combining cryptographic enforcement mechanisms with self-sovereign identity principles offers a promising approach for enabling fine-grained access control, data minimization, and progressive trust in decentralized data-sharing scenarios.

Traditional access control mechanisms, including access control lists and role-based access control, place the responsibility for evaluating and enforcing access policies entirely on service providers. This dependency introduces both technical and organizational risks, as policies may be misconfigured, bypassed, or deliberately ignored. While encryption is commonly employed to protect sensitive data stored by third parties, it is typically applied at rest and does not natively support fine-grained, recipient-specific, or selectively disclosed access to encrypted data. In addition, centralized key management introduces scalability and trust challenges.

To address these limitations and to empower users with greater control over their data in SSI environments, this chapter proposes a data-sharing model based on attribute-based encryption. In this model, the user constructs a *Data Capsule* that encapsulates an encrypted verifiable presentation together with a cryptographically bound access policy. The access policy is encoded directly into an attribute-based encryption ciphertext that protects a symmetric authorization secret, which is subsequently used to encrypt the capsule payload. Only service providers whose attribute-bound decryption keys satisfy the embedded access policy are able to recover the authorization secret and access the protected data.

4.2 Data Capsule

A Data Capsule is a privacy-preserving data exchange construct built upon CP-ABE and SSI primitives, including decentralized identifiers and verifiable credentials. The key advantages of the Data Capsule model are summarized as follows:

- It leverages decentralized identifiers and a ledger-backed registry to support decentralized discovery, transparency, and auditability of published access policy schemas, while verifiable credentials and presentations provide integrity and authenticity of disclosed claims.
- It introduces a structured mechanism for encrypting verifiable presentations, enabling selective disclosure while ensuring that disclosed claims remain confidential to unauthorized recipients.
- It encapsulates encrypted verifiable presentations together with cryptographically enforced access-control structures, enabling authorization decisions to be enforced at the cryptographic layer rather than by service-provider logic.

It leverages decentralized identifiers and a registry to support decen- tralized discovery, transparency, and auditability of published access policy schemas, while verifiable credentials and presentations provide integrity and authenticity of disclosed claims. It introduces a structured mechanism for encrypting verifiable presentations, enabling selective disclosure while ensuring that disclosed claims remain confidential to unau- thorized recipients. It encapsulates encrypted verifiable presentations together with cryptographically en- forced access-control structures, enabling authorization decisions to be enforced at the cryptographic layer rather than by service-provider logic

4.2.1 Case Study

Consider a national taxation system in which a government agency collects personal and financial information from citizens through an annual online submission process. Certain attributes such as name and address may be required immediately for identity verification and record matching, whereas detailed financial data may be processed later by a separate department (e.g., audit or compliance). This setting naturally motivates data minimization and progressive disclosure.

Regulatory frameworks reinforce this requirement. GDPR Recital 39 and Article 5(1)(c) [260] state that personal data must be adequate, relevant, and limited to what is necessary for the purposes for which they are processed, and that storage periods should be restricted to what is strictly necessary. However, in many existing systems, once data is submitted, it becomes broadly accessible within the internal infrastructure of the organization. Enforcement of purpose limitation therefore depends largely on administrative controls and application-layer access logic rather than cryptographic guarantees.

The proposed Data Capsule model enables a citizen to partition a tax submission into multiple cryptographically self-enforcing units, named capsules. For example, one capsule may contain identity attributes intended for immediate verification, while a second capsule may contain encrypted financial records protected under a stricter access policy applicable only to authorized audit personnel. Each capsule embeds its own access structure, ensuring that only entities whose certified attributes satisfy the policy can decrypt the protected data, independent of internal system configuration.

In the absence of DCs, a citizen wishing to encrypt their tax submission faces two suboptimal alternatives:

a) Encrypt the entire dataset and share the decryption capability with the entire agency, thereby granting broad access to all submitted information regardless of functional separation.

b) Retain exclusive control of the decryption key and decrypt data on an ad hoc basis for each departmental request. While this approach preserves user-side control, it requires continuous user involvement and does not scale in automated administrative workflows.

The Data Capsule model resolves this tension by enabling fine-grained, policy-bound, and cryptographically enforced disclosure without requiring ongoing user participation or blanket institutional trust.

4.3 Building Blocks

This section reviews the established cryptographic and self-sovereign identity primitives upon which the proposed Data Capsule construction is built.

4.3.1 SSI Framework

As described in Chapter 2, decentralized identifiers are a foundational component of self-sovereign identity architectures. The DID specification defines a globally unique, cryptographically verifiable identifier that can be resolved to a DID Document containing public keys and service endpoints. DIDs can be anchored and managed using decentralized infrastructures such as distributed ledgers, and ownership of a DID can be demonstrated through standard challenge–response protocols.

To reiterate from Chapter 2, a *Verifiable Credential* is an interoperable data structure for representing cryptographically verifiable and tamper-evident claims. A *Verifiable Presentation* is derived from one or more verifiable credentials and is constructed by a holder for disclosure to a specific verifier. VPs enable selective disclosure of claims and allow holders to control which attributes are shared in a given interaction.

The VC data model supports a *Terms of Use* property [261], which can be added by an issuer or a holder to communicate intended usage constraints. However, these terms are not cryptographically enforced after disclosure; compliance is largely procedural and contractual. Enforcement therefore depends on the behavior and trustworthiness of relying parties. The Data Capsule model addresses this limitation by enforcing access conditions directly at the cryptographic layer, independent of service-provider behavior.

As described in earlier chapters, Hyperledger Indy is a public-permissioned distributed ledger platform designed to support SSI use cases. While the proposed model is not specific to any single ledger technology, Hyperledger Indy is used in this chapter as a representative platform due to its native support for decentralized identifiers, credential schemas, and revocation registries, as well as its emphasis on interoperability and privacy-by-design principles.

4.3.2 Attribute-Based Encryption

Attribute-based encryption provides a cryptographic mechanism for enforcing fine-grained access control over encrypted data. In ABE systems, decryption is permitted only if a predefined access policy is satisfied by a set of attributes associated with the decryption key.

Two primary variants of ABE are commonly studied: ciphertext-policy ABE (CP-ABE) and key-policy ABE (KP-ABE). In KP-ABE, the decryption key embeds the access policy, while the ciphertext is associated with a set of attributes. In contrast, CP-ABE associates the access policy with the ciphertext and embeds attribute sets into decryption keys. Formal definitions of both constructions are provided by Goyal et al. [262], and the security model for CP-ABE is further developed by Waters [263].

The DC model adopts CP-ABE, as it allows data owners to define access policies at encryption time while enabling trusted authorities to issue attribute-bound decryption keys to service providers.

4.3.3 Underlying Algorithms

The ABE schemes used in the DC model are constructed using bilinear pairings and linear secret-sharing schemes (LSSS) [262]. The access control semantics follow an attribute-based access control (ABAC) model [39], in which authorization policies are expressed as Boolean formulas over a set of attributes.

Following Beimel et al. [264], let $\{P_1, P_2, \ldots, P_n\}$ denote a set of parties (or, in this context, attributes). A collection $\mathbb{A} \subseteq 2^{\{P_1,P_2,\ldots,P_n\}}$ is called *monotone* if for all B, C, whenever $B \in \mathbb{A}$ and $B \subseteq C$, it follows that $C \in \mathbb{A}$. An access structure is defined as a non-empty collection of authorized subsets:

$$\mathbb{A} \subseteq 2^{\{P_1,P_2,\ldots,P_n\}} \setminus \{\emptyset\}.$$

In the proposed model, access policies are restricted to monotone access structures, and $\mathbb{A}$ represents the set of authorized attribute combinations. These access structures are encoded as LSSS matrices using standard transformations [264, 263]. An access tree with l nodes results in an LSSS matrix with l rows.

A linear secret-sharing scheme Π over a set of parties $\mathbb{P}$ is defined over a finite field $\mathbb{Z}_p$ such that:

a) The shares distributed to each party form vectors over $\mathbb{Z}_p$.

b) There exists a share-generating matrix $\mathbb{M}$ with l rows and n columns. Given a secret $s \in \mathbb{Z}_p$ and random values $r_2, \ldots, r_n \in \mathbb{Z}_p$, the vector $v = (s, r_2, \ldots, r_n)$ produces shares $\mathbb{M}v$, where each row is associated with a specific attribute.

Bilinear pairings are used to enable policy evaluation during decryption. Let $\mathbb{G}_1$ and $\mathbb{G}_2$ be cyclic groups of prime order p with generators g_1 and g_2, and let $\mathbb{G}_T$ be a cyclic group of the same order. A bilinear map is a function

$$e : \mathbb{G}_1 \times \mathbb{G}_2 \rightarrow \mathbb{G}_T$$

satisfying bilinearity, non-degeneracy, and efficient computability.

A bilinear map $e : \mathbb{G}_1 \times \mathbb{G}_2 \rightarrow \mathbb{G}_T$ satisfies the following properties:

- Bilinearity: For all $u \in \mathbb{G}_1$, $v \in \mathbb{G}_2$, and $a, b \in \mathbb{Z}_p$, $e(u^a, v^b) = e(u, v)^{ab}$.
- Non-degeneracy: $e(g_1, g_2) \neq 1_{\mathbb{G}_T}$.
- Efficient computability: There exists a polynomial-time algorithm to compute $e(u, v)$ for all $u \in \mathbb{G}_1$, $v \in \mathbb{G}_2$.

4.3.4 Hybrid Encryption and Cryptographic Binding

The DC model employs a hybrid encryption strategy to enforce both fine-grained authorization and explicit recipient binding at the cryptographic layer. Attribute-based encryption is used to protect a short authorization secret, while public-key cryptography associated with decentralized identifiers is used to bind the capsule to a specific service provider. These two mechanisms are intentionally decoupled and later recombined to enforce dual cryptographic gating, ensuring that access to protected data requires simultaneous satisfaction of authorization and recipient identity constraints.

Rather than encrypting large payloads directly with public-key cryptography, which is inefficient for elliptic-curve and pairing-based systems, the DC model encrypts only small keying material using asymmetric primitives. A symmetric key derived via a key derivation function is then used to encrypt the Verifiable Presentation. This hybrid approach is widely adopted in secure messaging and data encapsulation protocols due to its efficiency and scalability [265, 266].

To cryptographically bind authorization and recipient identity, the DC model derives the final payload encryption key using the HMAC-based Extract-and-Expand Key Derivation Function (HKDF) [267]. Specifically, a secret recovered via CP-ABE decryption and a recipient-bound secret recovered via DID-based public-key decryption are combined to derive the payload key. This key is used exclusively to encrypt and decrypt the VP payload, ensuring that successful decryption is possible only when both authorization and recipient binding conditions are met.

The VP is encrypted using an authenticated encryption with associated data (AEAD) scheme, such as AES-GCM [268]. Selected metadata fields, including the recipient identifier, policy schema reference, capsule version, and cryptographic suite identifiers, are supplied as associated data. While this metadata remains in plaintext to support routing and auditability, AEAD guarantees that any modification to these fields is detected during decryption, providing integrity and contextual binding between the payload and its metadata.

4.4 Proposed Model

There are four main actors within the proposed model. A data owner (DO) is a user who possesses personal data and controls its disclosure. A service provider (SP) is an entity that consumes personal data subject to access restrictions. An attribute authority that can verify SP and issue keys. Finally, a decentralized registry, such as a blockchain-based framework, is used to enable decentralized trust by publishing decentralized identifiers and access policy schema. Figure 4.1 depicts the interplay among the four actors.

4.4.1 Components

The structure of a Data Capsule consists of three logically distinct layers:

a) **Metadata Layer:** Contains the Data Capsule version, identifiers of the cryptographic

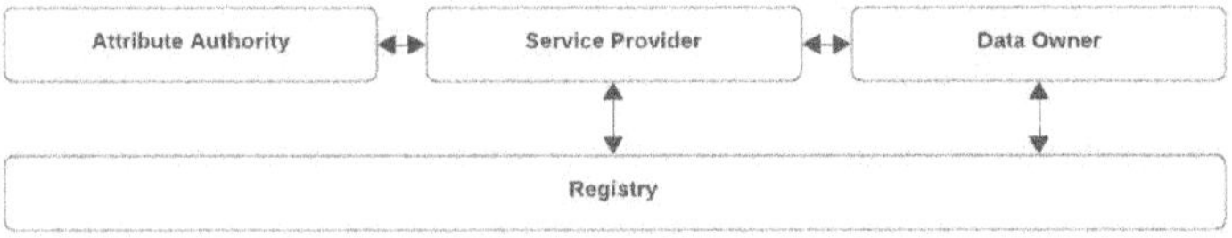

Figure 4.1: The four actors involved and their interactions in the proposed model

algorithms used, references to relevant registries, and a reference to the applied access policy schema (e.g., schema identifier and version). The metadata is transmitted in cleartext to support routing and policy discovery, and is integrity-protected by inclusion as associated authenticated data (AAD) during symmetric encryption.

b) **Protected Payload Layer:** Contains an encrypted Verifiable Presentation CT_{VP}. The VP is encrypted using authenticated symmetric encryption under a derived key k_{vp}. This layer ensures confidentiality and integrity of selectively disclosed claims.

c) **Key Protection Layer:** Contains two ciphertexts:

- a CP-ABE ciphertext CT_{ABE} protecting a secret key k_{abe} under an access policy; and
- a recipient-binding ciphertext CT_{bind} protecting a secret key k_{bind} under the service providers DID public key.

These ciphertexts jointly enforce attribute-based authorization and recipient binding.

4.4.2 Cryptographic Algorithms

We formalize the Data Capsule construction using standard cryptographic notation. The model consists of the following algorithms:

- **Setup**$(1^\lambda) \rightarrow (PK, MSK)$: Initializes the CP-ABE system. Given the security parameter λ, the algorithm outputs the public parameters PK and the master secret key MSK. The master secret key is held by trusted attribute authorities and is used exclusively for issuing attribute-bound decryption keys.

- **KeyGen**$(MSK, S) \to SK_S$: Generates a CP-ABE secret key for a service provider. Given the master secret key MSK and a verified attribute set S, the algorithm outputs a secret key SK_S bound to those attributes.
- **ABE-Encrypt**$(PK, A, k_{\text{abe}}) \to CT_{\text{ABE}}$: Encrypts a secret value k_{abe} under an access policy A using CP-ABE. Only keys whose attributes satisfy A can recover k_{abe}.
- **ABE-Decrypt**$(PK, CT_{\text{ABE}}, SK_S) \to k_{\text{abe}}$ or $\perp$: Recovers k_{abe} if and only if the attribute set embedded in SK_S satisfies the access policy encoded in CT_{ABE}.
- **Bind-Encrypt**$(PK_I, k_{\text{bind}}) \to CT_{\text{bind}}$: Encrypts a recipient-binding secret k_{bind} under the service providers DID public key PK_I using public-key encryption. Only the holder of the corresponding DID private key can recover k_{bind}.
- **Bind-Decrypt**$(sk_I, CT_{\text{bind}}) \to k_{\text{bind}}$ or $\perp$: Decrypts the recipient-binding ciphertext using the DID private key sk_I. Successful decryption constitutes a non-interactive proof of possession of the private key associated with the service providers DID.
- **KDF**$(k_{\text{abe}}, k_{\text{bind}}) \to k_{\text{vp}}$: Derives the final Verifiable Presentation encryption key using a standard key derivation function. This step enforces cryptographic gating: both authorization and recipient identity are required to derive k_{vp}.
- **Sym-Encrypt**$(k_{\text{vp}}, VP, Meta) \to CT_{\text{VP}}$: Encrypts the Verifiable Presentation using authenticated symmetric encryption (e.g., AES-GCM) under k_{vp}, with $Meta$ included as associated authenticated data (AAD).
- **Sym-Decrypt**$(k_{\text{vp}}, CT_{\text{VP}}, Meta) \to VP$ or $\perp$: Decrypts CT_{VP} under k_{vp} using $Meta$ as AAD.

- **Verify**$(VP) \rightarrow \{\text{valid}, \text{invalid}\}$: Verifies signatures and cryptographic proofs in the recovered VP using public keys resolved from decentralized identifiers.

The CP-ABE secret key SK_S and the DID private key sk_I serve orthogonal purposes authorization and identity binding while HKDF cryptographically enforces their joint requirement.

4.4.3 Model Execution

The execution of the proposed model is divided into two phases: (i) a system setup phase, and (ii) a Data Capsule generation phase.

System Setup Phase

a) The service provider generates a decentralized identifier and associated cryptographic key pair, and publishes its DID document to the decentralized registry.

b) The service provider publishes an access policy schema to the registry and references it from its DID document for decentralized discovery.

c) Attribute authorities execute **Setup**(1^λ) to initialize the CP-ABE system and retain the master secret key MSK.

d) Attribute authorities execute **KeyGen**(MSK, S) to issue a CP-ABE secret key SK_S to the service provider.

Data Capsule Generation

a) The data owner initiates an interaction with the service provider.

b) The data owner resolves the service providers DID to obtain PK_I and retrieves the referenced access policy schema.

c) The access policy schema is instantiated into a concrete Boolean access policy A.

d) The data owner constructs a Verifiable Presentation VP from selected Verifiable Credentials in their possession.

e) The data owner samples two fresh secrets:

$$k_{\text{abe}} \xleftarrow{\$} \{0,1\}^{\lambda}, \qquad k_{\text{bind}} \xleftarrow{\$} \{0,1\}^{\lambda}.$$

f) The data owner protects k_{abe} under the access policy:

$$\textbf{ABE-Encrypt}(PK, A, k_{\text{abe}}) \rightarrow CT_{\text{ABE}}.$$

g) The data owner encrypts k_{bind} under the service providers DID public key:

$$\textbf{Bind-Encrypt}(PK_I, k_{\text{bind}}) \rightarrow CT_{\text{bind}}.$$

h) The data owner derives the VP encryption key:

$$k_{\text{vp}} = \textbf{KDF}(k_{\text{abe}}, k_{\text{bind}}).$$

i) The capsule metadata structure, denoted by $Meta$, is constructed and the Verifiable Presentation is encrypted:

$$\textbf{Sym-Encrypt}(k_{\text{vp}}, VP, Meta) \rightarrow CT_{\text{VP}}.$$

j) The Data Capsule is assembled as:

$$DC = \{Meta,\ CT_{\text{ABE}},\ CT_{\text{bind}},\ CT_{\text{VP}}\},$$

and transmitted to the service provider.

k) Upon receipt, the service provider executes:

(a) **Bind-Decrypt**$(sk_I, CT_{\text{bind}}) \to k_{\text{bind}}$; abort if $\perp$.

(b) **ABE-Decrypt**$(PK, CT_{\text{ABE}}, SK_S) \to k_{\text{abe}}$; abort if $\perp$.

(c) $k_{\text{vp}} =$ **KDF**$(k_{\text{abe}}, k_{\text{bind}})$.

(d) **Sym-Decrypt**$(k_{\text{vp}}, CT_{\text{VP}}, Meta) \to VP$; abort if $\perp$.

(e) **Verify**(VP).

4.4.4 Security Considerations

This section analyzes the security properties of the proposed Data Capsule model and its underlying cryptographic components. We first describe the assumed threat model and identify the intended security goals of the construction. We then provide an informal security argument explaining why the design achieves policy soundness, recipient binding, collusion resistance, integrity, and confidentiality under standard cryptographic assumptions. Finally, we formalize confidentiality using an IND-CCA2 security model and provide a hybrid argument showing that the construction inherits its security from the underlying cryptographic primitives.

Threat Model

Although the data owner specifies access policies and performs capsule encryption, possession of the CP-ABE master secret key is intentionally excluded. The master secret key enables issuance of attribute-bound decryption keys, which represent externally verifiable claims about service providers. Allowing data owners to generate such keys would undermine the trust semantics of attributes and collapse the separation between policy definition and attribute attestation. In a full deployment, the master secret key may be distributed across multiple authorities using threshold cryptography or replaced by a multi-authority CP-ABE construction aligned with verifiable credential issuers.

We assume an adversary capable of the following:

- **Capsule Interception:** The adversary may obtain a copy of a Data Capsule during transmission or from storage.
- **Key Exposure Attempts:** The adversary may obtain or generate decryption keys corresponding to attribute sets that do *not* satisfy the embedded access policy.
- **Service Provider Compromise:** A malicious or compromised service provider may attempt to decrypt a capsule outside its authorized attribute set.
- **Collusion:** Multiple unauthorized service providers may combine their keys in an attempt to satisfy the access structure.

We assume the adversary cannot break the following standard cryptographic assumptions with non-negligible advantage:

- The q-parallel Bilinear Diffie-Hellman Exponent (q-BDHE) assumption underlying CP-ABE security [263]
- Indistinguishability under Chosen-Plaintext Attack (IND-CPA) and Integrity of Ciphertexts (INT-CTXT) security of AES-GCM [269, 268],
- unforgeability of digital signatures used to authenticate Verifiable Credentials,
- correctness and security of LSSS used to encode access structures [264].

Security Goals

The Data Capsule model is designed to satisfy the following security properties:

- **Policy Soundness:** Attribute sets that do not satisfy the policy must always result in decryption failure.
- **Recipient Binding:** Capsules are cryptographically bound to a specific service provider.

- **Collusion Resistance:** Unauthorized service providers cannot combine attributes across keys to satisfy a policy.
- **Integrity:** Any modification to the encrypted payload or associated metadata is detected during decryption.
- **Confidentiality:** Only recipients whose attributes satisfy the embedded access policy and who possess the intended recipient private key can decrypt the capsule.

Security Argument

We now provide an informal argument for why the Data Capsule construction achieves its intended security properties.

Policy Soundness Let S denote the attribute set embedded in a service providers CP-ABE secret key. CP-ABE guarantees that decryption of the authorization secret succeeds if and only if S satisfies the access structure encoded in the ciphertext, which is represented as an LSSS matrix [264]. If S does not satisfy the policy, decryption fails, preventing derivation of the payload key.

Recipient Binding Recipient binding is enforced by encrypting a binding secret under the service providers DID public key and incorporating this secret into the payload key derivation. This ensures that capsules cannot be replayed, forwarded, or substituted between service providers. Even an entity that satisfies the access policy cannot decrypt the capsule without possession of the corresponding DID private key.

Collusion Resistance CP-ABE schemes are designed to be resistant to key-collusion attacks. Independently randomized key components and the algebraic structure of bilinear pairings prevent multiple unauthorized parties from combining attributes across different keys to reconstruct a satisfying attribute set. Consequently, collusion between service providers does not enable unauthorized decryption. Collusion resistance follows directly from the security of the underlying CP-ABE construction and is inherited rather than separately proven here; we refer the reader to Waters [263] for the formal proof.

Integrity Integrity of the Data Capsule is provided at two levels: (i) integrity of the encrypted VP payload and capsule metadata, and (ii) integrity/authenticity of the verifiable credentials and proofs inside the decrypted VP.

First, the payload ciphertext CT_{VP} is produced using an authenticated encryption with associated data (AEAD). The capsule metadata $Meta$ is included as associated authenticated data (AAD) during encryption. Therefore, any adversarial modification of either (a) the ciphertext, (b) the nonce, or (c) any authenticated metadata field causes the decryption function to output $\perp$ except with negligible probability under INT-CTXT security of AEAD [270, 269, 268]. This prevents tampering, substitution, downgrade of cryptographic parameters, or re-binding a capsule to a different recipient or policy reference without detection.

Second, after successful decryption, the service provider executes **Verify**(VP), which validates issuer signatures (and any selective-disclosure proofs) over the verifiable credential content using public keys resolved from issuer DIDs. Under standard unforgeability assumptions for digital signatures, an adversary cannot modify claims inside the VC/VP without invalidating the corresponding proofs. Thus, the construction ensures that (i) ciphertext-level integrity protects the capsule as a transport object, and (ii) SSI proof verification preserves semantic integrity and authenticity of the disclosed claims once recovered.

Confidentiality

We first provide an informal justification of confidentiality. A formal proof is given in the next subsection. The payload is encrypted using symmetric authenticated encryption under a payload key k_{vp}. This key is derived via HKDF from two independent secrets:

$$k_{\text{vp}} = \text{HKDF}(k_{\text{abe}} \parallel k_{\text{bind}})$$

The authorization secret k_{abe} is protected under CP-ABE according to the access policy, while the recipient-binding secret k_{bind} is encrypted using hybrid public key encryption (HPKE) with the service providers DID public key.

Confidentiality follows from:

- IND-CPA security of CP-ABE under the decisional q-parallel Bilinear DiffieHellman Exponent (q-BDHE) assumption, as shown in Waters construction [263],
- IND-CPA and INT-CTXT security of AES-GCM [270],
- Indistinguishability under Chosen-Ciphertext Attack (IND-CCA2) security of HPKE instantiated with X25519 [271], HKDF-SHA256, and AES-256-GCM, as specified in RFC 9180 [272]

HKDF securely combines the two secrets to derive the payload key.

Formal Confidentiality Model

We now formalize the confidentiality of the Data Capsule construction using an *IND-CCA2* security game (indistinguishability under adaptive chosen-ciphertext attacks) [273]. The goal is to show that an adversary who obtains a challenge capsule and is allowed to make adaptive decryption queries on other capsules cannot determine which of two verifiable presentation payloads was encrypted even when the adversary can obtain CP-ABE attribute keys that do *not* satisfy the challenge policy and can query decryption of full capsules (except the challenge one).

We adopt the IND-CCA2 security model to capture a strong notion of confidentiality for the DC construction. The DC system operates in an open and potentially adversarial environment where encrypted capsules may be intercepted, replayed, or modified by malicious parties. Under such conditions, an adversary may attempt adaptive attacks by manipulating ciphertexts and observing system responses. The IND-CCA2 model reflects this threat scenario by allowing adaptive decryption queries while preventing trivial decryption of the challenge ciphertext. This ensures that the confidentiality of the protected payload remains preserved even in the presence of sophisticated ciphertext manipulation attacks.

Formally, we define the *DC-IND-CCA2* experiment between a challenger $\mathcal{C}$ and a probabilistic polynomial-time adversary $\mathcal{A}$:

- **Setup.** $\mathcal{C}$ runs the system setup (CP-ABE Setup, publishes public parameters PK), generates a recipient DID key pair (sk_I, PK_I), and gives PK and PK_I to $\mathcal{A}$.
- **Phase 1.** $\mathcal{A}$ may adaptively make the following queries:
  - CP-ABE key queries: $\mathcal{A}$ submits an attribute set S and receives $SK_S \leftarrow \textbf{KeyGen}(MSK, S)$.
  - Capsule decryption queries: $\mathcal{A}$ submits a full capsule $DC = (\textit{Meta}, CT_{\text{ABE}}, CT_{\text{bind}}, CT_{\text{VP}})$ (with *Meta* containing PK_I and policy reference). $\mathcal{C}$ runs the full decryption procedure and returns the recovered VP or $\perp$.
- **Challenge.** $\mathcal{A}$ submits a challenge policy A^*, two equal-length VPs: VP_0, VP_1, and associated metadata *Meta**.
  $\mathcal{C}$ picks random bit $b \xleftarrow{\$} \{0,1\}$, samples fresh $k_{\text{abe}}, k_{\text{bind}} \xleftarrow{\$} \{0,1\}^{256}$, and computes:
  $CT_{\text{ABE}} \leftarrow \textbf{ABE-Encrypt}(PK, A^*, k_{\text{abe}})$,
  $CT_{\text{bind}} \leftarrow \textbf{HPKE-Encrypt}(PK_I, k_{\text{bind}})$,
  $k_{\text{vp}} = \textbf{HKDF}(k_{\text{abe}} \parallel k_{\text{bind}})$,
  $CT_{\text{VP}} \leftarrow \textbf{AES-GCM-Enc}(k_{\text{vp}}, VP_b, \textit{Meta}^*)$,
  and returns the challenge capsule: $DC^* = (\textit{Meta}^*, CT_{\text{ABE}}, CT_{\text{bind}}, CT_{\text{VP}})$.
- **Phase 2.** Same as Phase 1, except $\mathcal{A}$ cannot submit the challenge capsule DC^* to

the decryption oracle, and CP-ABE key queries must satisfy $S \not\models A^*$. The restriction $S \not\models A^*$ ensures that the adversary cannot obtain a CP-ABE secret key whose attributes satisfy the challenge access policy, which would trivially allow decryption of the authorization secret.

- **Guess.** $\mathcal{A}$ outputs $b' \in \{0, 1\}$. $\mathcal{A}$ wins if $b' = b$.

The advantage of $\mathcal{A}$ is

$$^{\text{DC-IND-CCA2}}_{\mathcal{A}}(\lambda) = \left| \Pr[b' = b] - \frac{1}{2} \right|.$$

The Data Capsule scheme is IND-CCA2-secure if this advantage is negligible for every PPT $\mathcal{A}$.

Assuming (i) IND-CPA security of the CP-ABE scheme, (ii) IND-CCA2 security of HPKE, (iii) Pseudorandom function (PRF) security of HKDF, and (iv) AEAD Security (IND-CPA and INT-CTXT) of AES-GCM, the Data Capsule construction is IND-CCA2 secure.

The IND-CCA2 guarantee does not require CP-ABE to be IND-CCA2-secure. Rather, the decryption oracle is neutralized by the INT-CTXT property of AES-GCM and the IND-CCA2 property of HPKE before the ABE layer is exposed.

Proof Sketch (Hybrid Argument)

Let $\mathcal{A}$ be a probabilistic polynomial time (PPT) adversary against the DC-IND-CCA2 game. We define a sequence of hybrid games $\mathsf{H}_0, \mathsf{H}_1, \mathsf{H}_2, \mathsf{H}_3, \mathsf{H}_4$, where H_0 is the real game and H_4 is independent of the challenge bit b. We bound the distinguishing advantage between consecutive hybrids.

H_0 (Real game) Exactly the DC-IND-CCA2 experiment.

H_1 (Randomize HPKE-encapsulated secret) Replace the recipient-binding secret used in the challenge capsule with an independent random value $k'_{\text{bind}} \xleftarrow{\$} \{0, 1\}^{256}$ and recompute the HPKE ciphertext as $CT^*_{\text{bind}} \leftarrow$ **HPKE-Encrypt**(PK_I, k'_{bind}). The rest of the capsule construction remains unchanged. The decryption oracle continues to execute the standard decryption procedure.

H_2 (Randomize CP-ABE-encapsulated secret) Replace k_{abe} with independent uniform random $k'_{\text{abe}} \xleftarrow{\$} \{0,1\}^{256}$ in the challenge CT^*_{ABE}.

H_3 (Replace derived key with random) Replace k_{vp} with uniform random $\widehat{k} \xleftarrow{\$} \{0,1\}^{256}$ (independent of $k_{\text{abe}}, k_{\text{bind}}$) for the challenge CT^*_{VP}.

H_4 (Remove challenge bit dependence) Always encrypt VP_0 under $\widehat{k}$ in the challenge capsule.

The hybrids are indistinguishable under the following reductions:

- $|\Pr[\mathsf{H}_0 \Rightarrow 1] - \Pr[\mathsf{H}_1 \Rightarrow 1]| \leq^{\text{IND-CCA2}}_{\text{HPKE}} (\lambda)$. HPKE is IND-CCA2-secure (RFC 9180 [272]; mechanized proofs in [274]). The decryption oracle simulates correctly because invalid CT_{bind} capsules are already rejected by HPKE (CCA2 property propagates to the full capsule).

- $|\Pr[\mathsf{H}_1 \Rightarrow 1] - \Pr[\mathsf{H}_2 \Rightarrow 1]| \leq^{\text{IND-CPA}}_{\text{CP-ABE}} (\lambda)$. Standard Waters-style CP-ABE is IND-CPA-secure under q-parallel-BDHE [263]. The adversary's CP-ABE key queries are restricted ($S \not\models A^*$). CP-ABE protects only a randomly sampled symmetric key rather than the payload directly. Therefore adaptive decryption queries cannot reveal information about the challenge message unless the adversary can both recover the CP-ABE secret and break the AEAD encryption of the payload. Moreover, because AES-GCM satisfies INT-CTXT, any adversarially modified capsule is rejected at decryption with overwhelming probability, neutralizing the decryption oracle before it reaches the ABE layer. Therefore IND-CPA security of CP-ABE is sufficient here

- $|\Pr[\mathsf{H}_2 \Rightarrow 1] - \Pr[\mathsf{H}_3 \Rightarrow 1]| \leq^{\text{PRF}}_{\text{HKDF}} (\lambda) + \mathsf{negl}(\lambda)$. HKDF is a secure randomness extractor and pseudorandom function under standard assumptions on HMAC-SHA256

[267]. Under the assumption that HKDF instantiated with HMAC-SHA256 behaves as a PRF, the output of HKDF is computationally indistinguishable from a uniformly random key for any adversary that does not know both input secrets. Since both k_{abe} and k_{bind} remain hidden inside semantically secure ciphertexts, the derived key k_{vp} is indistinguishable from random.

- $|\Pr[\mathsf{H}_3 \Rightarrow 1] - \Pr[\mathsf{H}_4 \Rightarrow 1]| \leq^{\text{IND-CPA}}_{\text{AES-GCM}}(\lambda) +^{\text{INT-CTXT}}_{\text{AES-GCM}}(\lambda)$. AES-GCM provides AEAD security, consisting of (IND-CPA and INT-CTXT [268, 275]. With a uniformly random key $\widehat{k}$, encryptions of VP_0 and VP_1 are computationally indistinguishable. The decryption oracle remains consistent because any invalid capsule is rejected by the AEAD integrity check (or earlier by HPKE).

In H_4 the challenge capsule is independent of b, so $\Pr[\mathsf{H}_4 \Rightarrow b' = b] = 1/2$. By the triangle inequality,

$$ {}^{\text{DC-IND-CCA2}}_{\mathcal{A}}(\lambda) \leq^{\text{IND-CCA2}}_{\text{HPKE}}(\lambda) +^{\text{IND-CPA}}_{\text{CP-ABE}}(\lambda) +^{\text{PRF}}_{\text{HKDF}}(\lambda) +^{\text{AEAD}}_{\text{AES-GCM}}(\lambda) + \mathsf{negl}(\lambda). $$

Each term is negligible under the stated assumptions. Thus the Data Capsule construction achieves IND-CCA2 confidentiality under the stated cryptographic assumptions. The confidentiality guarantees of the DC construction follow from Theorem 1 under standard cryptographic assumptions.

Limitations and Assumptions

The security guarantees of the Data Capsule model rely on the following assumptions:

- **Authority Key Protection:** Compromise of the CP-ABE master secret key undermines attribute-based authorization.

- **Correct Policy Publication:** Malicious or incorrect policy publication is out of scope for this prototype.

- **Issuer Key Integrity:** Compromise of issuer signing keys undermines Verifiable Credential authenticity.

We further omit the scenario of a curious but honest service provider who stores and later leaks the recovered VP. The proposed construction enforces access but not retention or redistribution of the plaintext VP once decrypted.

Within these constraints, the Data Capsule model provides strong cryptographic enforcement of fine-grained access control suitable for self-sovereign identity data-sharing scenarios.

4.5 Implementation

To demonstrate the feasibility of the proposed Data Capsule model, we describe a proof-of-concept reference implementation that captures the core cryptographic, policy, and data encapsulation logic. The implementation reflects the intended SSI architecture at both the logical and cryptographic levels, while relying on local components to emulate decentralized registries and selected network interactions. The prototype consists of a data owner agent, a service provider module, and a registry for decentralized identifiers and access policy schemas. Core functionalities are developed using Python-based SSI tooling aligned with Hyperledger Aries concepts for decentralized identifiers and agent-based interactions, together with a CP-ABE cryptographic library built on the Charm-Crypto framework. Although the prototype adopts Aries-compatible data models and DID structures, it does not depend on the Hyperledger Aries agent framework at runtime. The local registry emulates the DID resolution and policy schema retrieval functions that a production deployment would perform via a live distributed ledger, without affecting the cryptographic correctness of the construction.

4.5.1 Implementation Environment

The prototype was developed in Python and executed on a MacBook Pro (Apple M1 Pro, macOS Sonoma 14.5).

This implementation serves to verify that encrypted Verifiable Presentations can be securely packaged into self-contained Data Capsules, that access control can be enforced entirely at the cryptographic layer, and that recipient binding can be achieved without relying on service-provider-side enforcement logic.

4.5.2 Architecture

The system architecture comprises the following components, shown in Figure 4.2:

- **Data Owner Agent:** An SSI-compliant wallet-like application responsible for Data Capsule creation. The agent supports selective disclosure of Verifiable Credentials, construction of Verifiable Presentations, symmetric encryption of VP payloads, CP-ABE protection of encryption keys under access policies, recipient binding using decentralized identifiers, and capsule assembly.

- **Service Provider Module:** A component capable of receiving Data Capsules, performing recipient-bound decryption using its DID private key, recovering attribute-protected secrets using CP-ABE decryption keys, deriving final payload decryption keys via HKDF, and validating decrypted Verifiable Presentations.

- **Decentralized Registry:** An emulated registry that stores decentralized identifiers, DID documents, public keys, and access policy schemas. In the prototype, this registry is implemented using SQLite.

- **Attribute Authority:** An administrative component responsible for system setup, validation and publication of access policy schemas, and issuance of CP-ABE secret keys to service providers based on externally verified attribute sets.

4.5.3 Key Libraries and Tools

- **Charm-Crypto:** Used to implement CP-ABE, bilinear pairing operations, and LSSS-based access structures.
- **SQLite / Secure Memory Store:** A local data store used to emulate registry functionality and securely hold cryptographic artifacts during capsule creation.
- **Python Cryptography Libraries:** Used for authenticated symmetric encryption (AES-GCM), HKDF-based key derivation, JSON processing, and capsule serialization.

The implementation follows the algorithmic structure defined previously and consists of three deterministic phases: (i) cryptographic preparation and key provisioning, (ii) Data Capsule creation by the data owner, and (iii) Data Capsule decryption by the service provider. The prototype implements a hybrid construction in which the Verifiable Presentation is encrypted using AES-256-GCM, while access control and recipient binding are enforced by deriving the VP encryption key from two independent 256-bit secrets: an attribute-protected secret recovered via CP-ABE and a recipient-binding secret recovered via DID-based public-key encryption.

All cryptographic parameters required for correct decryption are explicitly encoded in the capsule metadata. The Data Capsule contains exactly the following four elements:

$$DC = \{Meta,\ CT_{\mathrm{VP}},\ CT_{\mathrm{ABE}},\ CT_{\mathrm{bind}}\}.$$

Preparation

Prior to Data Capsule creation and consumption, system-wide cryptographic setup and key provisioning are performed. These steps are executed once per deployment and are independent of individual capsule instances.

a) **CP-ABE system setup.** A trusted authority initializes the CP-ABE scheme by executing:

$$(PK, MK) \leftarrow \textbf{ABE-Setup}(1^\lambda),$$

where λ is the security parameter. The public parameters PK are distributed to all participants, while the master secret key MK is retained by the authority.

b) **Attribute key issuance.** For each service provider with certified attribute set S, the authority issues an attribute-bound CP-ABE secret key:

$$SK_S \leftarrow \textbf{ABE-KeyGen}(MK, S).$$

The secret key SK_S enables decryption of CP-ABE ciphertexts whose access policy is satisfied by S.

c) **DID key registration.** Each service provider generates an X25519 [271] key pair (sk_I, PK_I) for encryption. The public key PK_I is published in the providers DID Document, while the private key sk_I remains under the exclusive control of the provider.

Data Capsule Creation

a) **Local wallet authentication.** The data owner authenticates to the wallet application, unlocking access to stored Verifiable Credentials, cryptographic keys, and cached registry data.

b) **Resolve service provider DID.** The wallet resolves the service providers DID and retrieves the DID Document. From the document, the wallet extracts the X25519 public key PK_I used for recipient-binding encryption.

c) **Construct a selective-disclosure VP.** The wallet constructs a Verifiable Presentation VP containing only the claims required for the interaction, using selective disclosure over the underlying Verifiable Credentials.

d) **Instantiate the access policy.** The wallet instantiates a concrete Boolean access policy A from the referenced policy schema and converts it into a monotonic access structure compatible with CP-ABE.

e) **Generate authorization and binding secrets.** The wallet generates two independent uniformly random 256-bit secrets:

$$k_{\text{abe}} \xleftarrow{\$} \{0,1\}^{256}, \qquad k_{\text{bind}} \xleftarrow{\$} \{0,1\}^{256}.$$

f) **Encrypt the authorization secret with CP-ABE.** Using CP-ABE public parameters PK, the wallet encrypts k_{abe} under access policy A:

$$CT_{\text{ABE}} = \textbf{ABE-Encrypt}(PK, A, k_{\text{abe}}).$$

g) **Encrypt the binding secret using DID-based public-key encryption.** The wallet encrypts k_{bind} using Hybrid Public-Key Encryption (HPKE) [272] as the binding encryption function, with the service providers X25519 public key PK_I and the ciphersuite:

`HPKE-X25519-HKDF-SHA256-AES-256-GCM.`

The resulting ciphertext is:

$$CT_{\text{bind}} = \textbf{HPKE-Encrypt}(PK_I, k_{\text{bind}}).$$

h) **Derive the VP encryption key.** The wallet derives the VP encryption key using

HKDF-SHA-256:

$$
\begin{aligned}
k_{\text{vp}} = \textbf{HKDF\_SHA256}\big(\text{IKM} &= k_{\text{abe}} \parallel k_{\text{bind}}, \\
\text{salt} &= \texttt{Meta.hkdfSalt}, \\
\text{info} &= \texttt{Meta.hkdfInfo}, \\
L &= \texttt{Meta.hkdfLen}\big)
\end{aligned}
\tag{4.1}
$$

i) **Construct metadata.** The wallet constructs a metadata structure `Meta` containing:

- `version`: Data Capsule format version identifier.
- `cipherSuiteVP`: Symmetric cipher used to encrypt the VP payload
- `cipherSuiteBind`: Public-key encryption ciphersuite used for recipient binding
- `cipherSuiteABE`: ABE scheme identifier
- `recipientDID`: Decentralized identifier of the intended service provider.
- `policySchemaRef`: reference (DID fragment or URL) to the access policy schema used during encryption.
- `nonceVP`: A fresh nonce used for encryption of the verifiable presentation.
- `hkdfSalt`: Salt used in HKDF during payload-key derivation.
- `hkdfInfo`: Context string for HKDF domain separation
- `hkdfLen`: Output key length for HKDF
- `capsuleId`: A unique identifier for the capsule

j) **Encrypt the VP.** The wallet encrypts the serialized VP using AES-256-GCM under

k_{vp}, with `Meta` as associated data:

$$CT_{\text{VP}} = \text{AES-256-GCM-Enc}\big(k_{\text{vp}}, \texttt{Meta.nonceVP}, VP, \text{AAD} = \texttt{Meta}\big) \quad (4.2)$$

k) **Assemble and transmit the Data Capsule.** The Data Capsule is assembled as:

$$DC = \{\texttt{Meta},\ CT_{\text{VP}},\ CT_{\text{ABE}},\ CT_{\text{bind}}\}$$

and transmitted to the service provider.

Data Capsule Decryption

a) **Recover the recipient-binding secret.** Using its DID private key sk_I, the service provider decrypts:

$$k_{\text{bind}} = \textbf{HPKE-Decrypt}(sk_I, CT_{\text{bind}}).$$

b) **Recover the authorization secret via CP-ABE.** Using its attribute-bound secret key SK_S, the service provider decrypts:

$$k_{\text{abe}} = \textbf{ABE-Decrypt}(PK, CT_{\text{ABE}}, SK_S).$$

c) **Derive the VP decryption key.** The service provider derives:

$$k_{\text{vp}} = \textbf{HKDF\_SHA256}\big(\text{IKM} = k_{\text{abe}} \parallel k_{\text{bind}}, \text{salt} = \texttt{Meta.hkdfSalt}, \text{info} = \texttt{Meta.hkdfInfo}, L = \texttt{Meta.hkdfLen}\big) \quad (4.3)$$

d) **Decrypt and authenticate the VP.** The service provider decrypts:

$$VP = \textbf{AES-256-GCM-Dec}\big(k_{\text{vp}},\ \texttt{Meta.nonceVP},\ CT_{\text{VP}},\ \text{AAD} = \texttt{Meta}\big).$$

e) **Verify VP cryptographic proofs.** The service provider verifies issuer signatures and cryptographic proofs contained in the VP using public keys resolved from issuer DIDs.

4.5.4 Security Mechanisms in the Implementation

In the prototype, policy publication and retrieval are emulated using a local registry for experimental repeatability. Adversarial or incorrect policy publication is considered out of scope for this implementation.

The prototype enforces these goals through the following mechanisms:

- **Wallet Authentication:** Local authentication protects access to credentials and cryptographic keys within the wallet.
- **Attribute Isolation:** Each CP-ABE secret key encodes only the attributes authorized for a specific service provider.
- **Recipient Binding:** The Data Capsule enforces recipient binding by encrypting a dedicated binding secret under the service providers DID public key.
- **Policy Traceability:** Access policy schemas are referenced explicitly in capsule metadata. In a full deployment, these schemas would be published on a tamper-evident registry; in the prototype, this behavior is emulated locally.
- **Data Minimization:** Multiple Data Capsules can be generated from the same credentials, each containing a different selectively disclosed Verifiable Presentation.

4.6 Data Structures

In this section, we describe the key data structures used in the Data Capsule ecosystem and illustrate how they relate to one another. In particular, we present (i) the structure of a Data Capsule, (ii) the metadata fields required for routing, cryptographic interpretation, and auditability, (iii) a service provider DID and DID Document, (iv) an access policy schema published on a registry and referenced from the DID Document, (v) sample instantiated access policies used in the experiments, and (vi) sample verifiable credentials and verifiable presentations that are encrypted and packaged into Data Capsules.

A Data Capsule is a self-contained cryptographic container designed to support secure, policy-driven, and recipient-bound data exchange. A capsule consists of four primary elements:

- **Metadata** ($Meta$): Cleartext structural information required for routing, cryptographic interpretation, and policy traceability.
- **Encrypted Verifiable Presentation** (CT_{VP}): The selectively disclosed user data encrypted under a symmetric payload key.
- **CP-ABE Ciphertext** (CT_{ABE}): A ciphertext protecting an authorization secret under an attribute-based access policy.
- **Recipient Binding Ciphertext** (CT_{bind}): A ciphertext encrypting a binding secret under the service providers DID public key.

Formally, as shown in 4.2, a Data Capsule is represented as:

$$DC = \{Meta, CT_{\mathrm{VP}}, CT_{\mathrm{ABE}}, CT_{\mathrm{bind}}\}.$$

Access to the encrypted payload requires both possession of a CP-ABE secret key whose embedded attributes satisfy the access policy and possession of the private key corresponding to the recipients decentralized identifier.

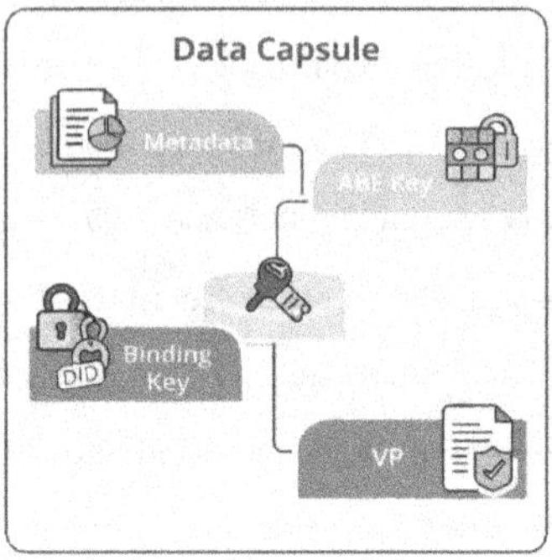

Figure 4.2: High-level structure of the Data Capsule

4.6.1 Structure of Metadata

The metadata component contains no personal data and is intentionally kept outside of public-key encryption. It provides the information required to correctly interpret, route, and verify the capsule contents.

A metadata record contains the following fields:

- `version`: `1.0`
- `cipherSuiteVP`: `AES-256-GCM`.
- `cipherSuiteBind`: `HPKE-X25519-HKDF-SHA256-AES-256-GCM`.
- `cipherSuiteABE`: `CP-ABE-WATERS11-SS512`.
- `recipientDID`: `did:indy:gov:tax-agency`.
- `policySchemaRef`: `did:indy:gov:tax-agency#policySchema-1`.

- `nonceVP`: Random 12 bytes, base64 encoded
- `hkdfSalt`: Random 16 bytes, base64 encoded
- `hkdfInfo`: `"DC-VP-Key-v1"`.
- `hkdfLen`: 32 (bytes)
- `capsuleId`: A unique identifier computed as:

$$\texttt{capsuleId} = H(Meta \parallel r),$$

  where r is a fresh random value and where $Meta$ denotes the metadata structure with the `capsuleId` field set to the empty string. This identifier is used for indexing and audit logs and is not required for cryptographic correctness.

The metadata enables auditability, policy traceability, and early rejection of capsules not intended for a given recipient.

4.6.2 DID and DID Document

In the proposed model, service providers are identified using decentralized identifiers. As described in Chapter 2, a DID resolves to a DID Document containing cryptographic verification material and service endpoints.

In the DC model, the DID Document additionally serves as a *policy discovery mechanism* by referencing the service providers access policy schema published on a decentralized registry. The DID Document also publishes the public key used for recipient binding encryption.

Listing 1 shows a sample service provider DID.

Listing 1: Sample service provider DID

```
did:indy:gov:tax-agency
```

Listing 2 shows a minimal DID Document containing a reference to the access policy schema. The document includes an Ed25519 verification key for authentication/signatures and an X25519 key agreement key for recipient binding encryption.


```
{
  "@context": "https://www.w3.org/ns/did/v1",
  "id": "did:indy:gov:tax-agency",
  "verificationMethod": [
    {
      "id": "did:indy:gov:tax-agency#key-sign-1",
      "type": "Ed25519VerificationKey2020",
      "controller": "did:indy:gov:tax-agency",
      "publicKeyMultibase": "z6Mki..."
    },
    {
      "id": "did:indy:gov:tax-agency#key-agree-1",
      "type": "X25519KeyAgreementKey2020",
      "controller": "did:indy:gov:tax-agency",
      "publicKeyMultibase": "z6LS..."
    }
  ],
  "authentication": [
    "did:indy:gov:tax-agency#key-sign-1"
  ],
  "keyAgreement": [
    "did:indy:gov:tax-agency#key-agree-1"
  ],
  "service": [
    {
      "id": "did:indy:gov:tax-agency#policy-schema-1",
      "type": "DataCapsuleAccessPolicySchema",
      "serviceEndpoint":
        ↪ "https://registry.gov.example/policies/tax-policy-schema-v1.json"
    }
  ]
}
```


Listing 2: Minimal DID Document referencing an access policy schema and an encryption key

During Data Capsule creation, the data owner resolves the service providers DID to obtain the DID public key used for recipient binding and the endpoint used to retrieve the access policy schema.

4.6.3 Access Policy Schema

Rather than publishing concrete Boolean expressions for each transaction, service providers publish an *access policy schema* that declaratively specifies authorization requirements. The schema defines the attribute vocabulary, a policy template, and the cryptographic parameters required by the Data Capsule construction.

Listing 3 shows an example access policy schema published by a tax authority.

```
{
  "id": "did:indy:gov:tax-agency#policySchema-1",
  "type": "DataCapsuleAccessPolicySchema",
  "version": "1.0",
  "policyLanguage": "boolean",
  "attributes": [
    "department",
    "role",
    "clearance"
  ],
  "policyTemplate": "(department='tax' AND (role='auditor' OR role='admin') AND
    ↪  clearance='level3')",
  "monotone": true,
   "crypto": {
  "supportedCipherSuiteVP": ["AES-256-GCM"],
  "supportedCipherSuiteBind": ["HPKE-X25519-HKDF-SHA256-AES-256-GCM"],
  "supportedCipherSuiteABE": ["CP-ABE-WATERS11-SS512"],
  "supportedKDF": ["HKDF-SHA256"]
   }
}
```

Listing 3: Example access policy schema published by a service provider

The schema expresses *authorization requirements* rather than attributes of the service provider itself. Attribute claims are cryptographically bound to CP-ABE secret keys issued by authoritative entities, preventing self-assertion and enabling externally verifiable authorization.

4.6.4 Access Policies Used in the Prototype

To evaluate authorization complexity, two concrete access policies were instantiated from the schema:

- **Simple Access Policy:**

```
(role = 'auditor' AND clearance = 'level1')
```

- **Complex Access Policy:**

```
(department = 'tax' AND
 (role = 'auditor' OR role = 'admin') AND
 clearance = 'level3')
```

These Boolean expressions were converted into LSSS matrices and embedded into CP-ABE ciphertexts protecting the authorization secret.

4.6.5 Policy Placement and Enforcement

Policy enforcement occurs at the cryptographic layer, while the Verifiable Presentation supports selective disclosure:

a) **Within the Verifiable Presentation:** Only the claims necessary for the specific service interaction are disclosed, supporting data minimization.

b) **Within CP-ABE Encryption:** The access policy is encoded as an LSSS matrix and embedded into the CP-ABE ciphertext.

Decryption succeeds only if the service providers CP-ABE secret key embeds an attribute set satisfying the access structure.

4.6.6 Verifiable Credentials and Presentations

The verifiable credential used in the experiments contains information commonly found in government tax filing records, including:

- Tax year
- Full legal name
- Residential address
- Filing identifier (e.g., return/record ID)
- Filing summary (e.g., total income, total deductions, and tax payable)

This information is selectively packaged into a verifiable presentation before encryption and encapsulation.

Sample Verifiable Credential

Figure 4.3 shows a sample verifiable credential representing personal and financial information.

Sample Verifiable Presentation

Figure 4.4 shows a verifiable presentation disclosing only the attributes required to satisfy the complex access policy.

4.7 Results

We evaluated the behavior, correctness, and performance characteristics of the proposed Data Capsule prototype using a local Python-based reference implementation. The experiments were designed to assess (i) cryptographic overhead introduced by CP-ABE-based access control, (ii) the impact of access policy complexity on latency and capsule size, (iii)

```
{
  "@context": [
    "https://www.w3.org/2018/credentials/v1"
  ],
  "type": [
    "VerifiableCredential",
    "TaxFilingCredential"
  ],
  "issuer": "did:indy:gov:tax-authority",
  "issuanceDate": "2025-01-20T00:00:00Z",
  "credentialSubject": {
    "id": "did:indy:user:67890",
    "taxYear": "2024",
    "fullName": "Jane Smith",
    "address": "123 Elm Street, Metropolis",
    "filingId": "TAX-2024-00019384",
    "summary": {
      "incomeTotal": 82000,
      "deductionsTotal": 12000,
      "taxPayable": 9400
    }
  },
  "proof": {
    "type": "Ed25519Signature2020",
    "created": "2025-01-20T00:00:00Z",
    "proofPurpose": "assertionMethod",
    "verificationMethod": "did:indy:gov:tax-authority#key-sign-1",
    "proofValue": "..."
  }
}
```

Figure 4.3: Sample Verifiable Credential representing a tax filing information issued by a government tax authority

```
{
  "@context": [
    "https://www.w3.org/2018/credentials/v1"
  ],
  "type": [
    "VerifiablePresentation"
  ],
  "holder": "did:indy:user:67890",
  "verifiableCredential": [
    {
      "type": [
        "VerifiableCredential",
        "TaxFilingCredential"
      ],
      "issuer": "did:indy:gov:tax-authority",
      "credentialSubject": {
        "id": "did:indy:user:67890",
        "taxYear": "2024",
        "filingId": "TAX-2024-00019384",
        "summary": {
          "incomeTotal": 82000,
          "deductionsTotal": 12000
        }
      }
    }
  ],
  "proof": {
    "type": "Ed25519Signature2020",
    "created": "2025-01-21T00:00:00Z",
    "proofPurpose": "authentication",
    "verificationMethod": "did:indy:user:67890#key-sign-1",
    "proofValue": "..."
  }
}
```


Figure 4.4: Selective-disclosure Verifiable Presentation containing only the user claims required for the service interaction the practical benefit of the hybrid design combining CP-ABE, recipient binding, and symmetric encryption, and (iv) the correctness of cryptographic access control enforcement.

4.7.1 Test Configuration

All experiments were executed locally using the reference implementation described earlier. The prototype was implemented in Python and relies on the `charm-crypto` library for CP-ABE operations and the `cryptography` library for authenticated symmetric encryption (AES-GCM) and HKDF-based key derivation. Recipient binding is implemented using an X25519-based construction as described in the implementation section.

Synthetic verifiable credentials were generated to emulate organizational identity attributes relevant to authorization policies (e.g., role, department, and clearance). Verifiable Presentations were constructed using selective disclosure and encrypted as part of Data Capsules. Two access policy configurations were evaluated:

- A *simple* policy involving a small number of attributes and no nested Boolean expressions.
- A *complex* policy representing a realistic authorization rule with multiple attributes and nested Boolean conditions.

All measurements were repeated 30 times, and the reported results correspond to averaged values. Since CP-ABE setup and attribute-key issuance are offline operations, runtime measurements focus on per-capsule encryption and decryption costs.

4.7.2 Key Generation Overhead

To evaluate the scalability of CP-ABE with respect to the size of a service providers attribute set, we measured the time required to generate CP-ABE decryption keys for increasing numbers of attributes. Table 4.1 summarizes the results.

The results confirm that CP-ABE key issuance scales approximately linearly with the num-

Number of Attributes in Key	KeyGen Time (ms)
1	4.8
3	7.20
5	9.55
10	16.33
20	29.83

Table 4.1: CP-ABE key generation time as a function of the number of attributes in the service providers decryption key (average of 30 runs).

ber of attributes, which is consistent with the underlying linear secret-sharing construction. Since key generation is performed infrequently during onboarding or credential issuance, this overhead does not affect per-capsule latency.

4.7.3 Encryption, Decryption, and Capsule Size

We measured end-to-end Data Capsule encryption and decryption latency for both access policy scenarios. Encryption time includes CP-ABE encryption of the authorization secret, recipient-binding encryption of the binding secret, HKDF-based payload key derivation, and AES-256-GCM encryption of the Verifiable Presentation. Decryption time includes recipient-binding decryption, CP-ABE decryption, key derivation, and authenticated AES-GCM decryption of the payload. Table 4.2 summarizes the results.

Operation	Simple Policy (ms)	Complex Policy (ms)
Encryption Time	12.16	20.83
Decryption Time	5.82	7.32
Capsule Size (KB)	3.15	4.04

Table 4.2: Data Capsule encryption/decryption latency and size (average of 30 runs).

CP-ABE operations are likely the primary contributors to the observed runtime overhead. Although individual component timings were not isolated in this experiment, this behavior is consistent with the higher computational cost of pairing-based cryptography compared to symmetric encryption and key derivation functions.

4.7.4 Impact of Policy Size on Latency

To isolate the effect of access policy complexity, we measured encryption and decryption latency as a function of the number of leaf nodes in the Boolean access structure. We measure latency based on the following four policies:

a) Policy 1 = "role:auditor"

b) Policy 2 = "(role:auditor and department:tax and clearance:level3)"

c) Policy 3 = "(role:auditor and department:tax and clearance:level3 and org:gov and region:on)"

d) Policy 4 = "(role:auditor and department:tax and clearance:level3 and org:gov and region:on and tier:t1 and purpose:audit)"

Each leaf corresponds to an atomic attribute condition and contributes to the size of the underlying LSSS matrix embedded in the CP-ABE ciphertext. Table 4.3 reports the results.

Policy Class	**Leaf Count**	**Enc. Time (ms)**	**Dec. Time (ms)**
Policy 1	1	7.46	4.53
Policy 2	3	16.33	6.93
Policy 3	5	25.13	9.42
Policy 4	7	34.30	11.81

Table 4.3: Encryption and decryption latency as a function of access policy leaf count (average of 30 runs).

The near-linear growth is consistent with the computational complexity of CP-ABE schemes based on linear secret-sharing, since each additional leaf introduces additional pairing operations during encryption and decryption.

4.7.5 Ciphertext Expansion with Policy Complexity

We next examined the effect of access policy complexity on Data Capsule size. As additional attributes are introduced into the access structure, the CP-ABE ciphertext grows due to additional group elements. Table 4.4 shows the resulting capsule size for policies of increasing complexity.

Policy Class	Leaf Count	Capsule Size (KB)
Policy 1	1	2.69
Policy 2	3	3.60
Policy 3	5	4.46
Policy 4	7	5.31

Table 4.4: Data Capsule size as a function of access policy complexity (average of 30 runs).

The measured growth confirms that capsule expansion is primarily driven by the CP-ABE ciphertext, while the encrypted VP payload and recipient-binding ciphertext remain approximately constant in size.

4.7.6 Access Control Correctness

Finally, we evaluated whether cryptographic access control correctly enforces the intended authorization semantics. Five service provider profiles with different attribute sets were tested against the complex tax policy. Table 4.5 summarizes the outcomes.

Service Provider Profile	Attributes	Decryption Result
SP1: Tax Auditor	department = tax, role = auditor, clearance = level3	Success
SP2: Tax Clerk	department = tax, role = clerk, clearance = level2	Failure
SP3: University Registrar	department = education, role = registrar, clearance = level2	Failure
SP4: System Administrator	department = it, role = admin, clearance = level1	Failure
SP5: Tax Admin	department = tax, role = admin, clearance = level3	Success

Table 4.5: Decryption results for different service provider attribute sets.

Only service providers whose attributes satisfied the access policy were able to recover both cryptographic secrets and derive the payload decryption key. All other profiles failed during CP-ABE decryption, demonstrating that access control is enforced entirely at the cryptographic layer without reliance on service-side authorization logic.

The experimental results show that the proposed Data Capsule model provides correct, scalable, and efficient cryptographic access control suitable for self-sovereign identity data-sharing scenarios.

4.8 Conclusion

This chapter presented a Data Capsule model for secure and privacy-preserving data sharing within self-sovereign identity ecosystems. The proposed design enables fine-grained, cryptographically enforced access control over selectively disclosed data, while maintaining a user-centric model that minimizes reliance on centralized intermediaries.

The Data Capsule construction combines policy-based authorization with recipient binding, ensuring that access is granted only when both the declared access requirements and the intended recipient identity are satisfied. By encapsulating these mechanisms within a single transferable container, the model supports controlled data exchange without requiring continuous user involvement or trusted third-party data custodians during each access request.

The related work surveyed earlier in this dissertation demonstrates a wide range of privacy-oriented data management approaches. In contrast, this chapter advances existing designs by tightly aligning attribute-based access control with self-sovereign identity principles, enabling policy-driven data sharing that is both cryptographically enforced and interoperable with decentralized identity infrastructures.

By requiring service providers to publish access policy schemas via decentralized registries, the proposed model improves transparency and auditability of authorization requirements and reduces ambiguity regarding intended data usage. The experimental evaluation confirms that the hybrid encryption design achieves acceptable performance while maintaining security guarantees, making the Data Capsule model suitable for real-world data-sharing scenarios.

Chapter 5

Leveraging Self-Sovereign Identity to Improve Know Your Customer

Over the past several years, SSI has been explored across a range of applications. In parallel, evolving expectations around Anti-Money Laundering (AML) compliance and Know Your Customer (KYC) procedures have increased interest in approaches that support reusable verification, stronger authentication, and more user-centric handling of identity data.

5.1 Introduction

As discussed in Chapter 2, the current identity management landscape prioritizes the needs of identity and service providers over those of identity owners. In this chapter, we develop a client onboarding framework named *KYC2*. Similar to the solutions proposed in previous chapters, this framework is based on Hyperledger Indy. Our framework simulates a financial client onboarding scenario in which a client registers in-person with a bank, obtains digital identity credentials from the bank and uses these credentials to digitally register and open a new account with a secondary bank. The simulation allows us to explore Hyperledger Indy, and SSI as a possible solution to address the challenges presented by the current identity management models and KYC procedures. The simulation is followed by an assessment of the KYC2 framework based on the principles of SSI, General Data Protection Regulation (GDPR) and Privacy by Design (PbD) [276]. While this chapter uses

Hyperledger Indy as the reference platform for the prototype, the core ideas in KYC2 of holder mediated disclosure, reusable verifiable proofs, and ledger-backed discovery of public verification material are not specific to any single implementation stack. The framework is therefore presented as an architectural pattern aligned with SSI principles rather than a platform-dependent solution.

There are several driving factors behind our proposed client onboarding framework. The introduction of GDPR, the challenges faced by underbanked and under-identified individuals, and the increasing cost of KYC are all key motivations for this framework.

5.1.1 GDPR

As discussed in Chapter 2, GDPR is the European Unions data protection framework, which took effect in May 2018. While the regulation primarily applies to EU residents, it also affects organizations outside the EU that collect or process personal data of EU residents. The introduction of GDPR necessitates solutions with strong security and privacy measures. Section 5.3 discusses key GDPR principles related to personal data.

5.1.2 Underbanked and Under-identified

The number of underbanked individuals living in rural areas without access to banking infrastructure is significant. Widely cited World Bank estimates suggest that approximately 2 billion people worldwide lack access to financial services [277]. The number of underbanked people living in urban centers in developed countries is also surprisingly high. A 2015 report suggests that 20% of U.S. households are underbanked [278], while a 2023 report suggest that over 14% of U. S. households were underbanked [279]. Financial inclusion has been emphasized as an important global priority [280].

5.1.3 Open Banking and Third Party Financial Services

Open Banking initiatives have emerged as a key driver of innovation in the financial sector by enabling regulated third-party providers to access customer financial data through standardized and secure APIs [281]. This model promotes competition, enhances customer choice, and enables the development of value-added services such as account aggregation, credit scoring, and personalized financial management tools. Despite these advancements, Open Banking primarily addresses data portability and service interoperability, while leaving identity verification processes largely unchanged. Clients are still required to undergo repeated Know Your Customer procedures across third-party providers. Beyond identity verification, controlled data sharing plays a central role in enabling user-centric services within the financial ecosystem. Traditional data sharing models rely on centralized platforms that aggregate and redistribute user data, often without granular control or transparency for the user. In contrast, a user-centric approach enables individuals to share only the minimum necessary informationpotentially in the form of verifiable proofsthereby reducing unnecessary data exposure while maintaining trust in the authenticity of the shared information. These challenges and opportunities necessitate the exploration of an interoperable, multi-jurisdictional, and scalable identity management system that is accessible to populations without easy access to brick-and-mortar financial institutions.

5.1.4 Cost of Know Your Customer (KYC)

Know Your Customer (KYC) is the process through which financial institutions engage with prospective clients to verify their identity [282]. Through this process, banks gain better insight into their clients and establish a rapport that helps them understand how their clients funds are obtained, accessed, and withdrawn. KYC is especially important for politically exposed persons (PEPs), high-risk individuals, and individuals subject to sanctions. KYC is a necessary process to prevent money laundering and terrorism financing.

The cost of complying with KYC and anti-money laundering (AML) regulations increases each year. Banks that fail to comply with these regulations face severe penalties and, in extreme cases, restrictions on their operations. On the other hand, KYC is often a slow, inconvenient, and sometimes insecure process for clients [283]. A typical client registration process involves the manual submission of physical identity documents, which can be easily forged or lost. Furthermore, banks are sometimes organized into product silos, increasing the complexity of the onboarding process. These issues highlight the need for an overhaul in the way we implement the KYC process.

5.2 Framework of KYC2

The KYC2 framework introduces an identity management ecosystem in which the identity data of users (i.e., banking clients) are stored in their digital wallet. The banks enrolled in the KYC2 ecosystem can issue Verifiable Credentials to clients once their identities are successfully verified. Subsequent identity verifications and account creations can be accomplished by having the client disclose previously issued credentials to the banks. The client retains primary control over when and what credentials are disclosed, and no identity data is communicated to the banks without the clients explicit participation and consent.

5.2.1 Architecture

The KYC2 architecture consists of three components:

a) The banks A and B

b) Bank client Q

c) Validator nodes 1, 2, 3, and 4

As shown in Figure 5.1, the client and the banks each have an agent and a wallet. Four validator nodes are responsible for managing the distributed ledger. For the system to tolerate at least one Byzantine fault in Hyperledger Indy, there must be at least four validator

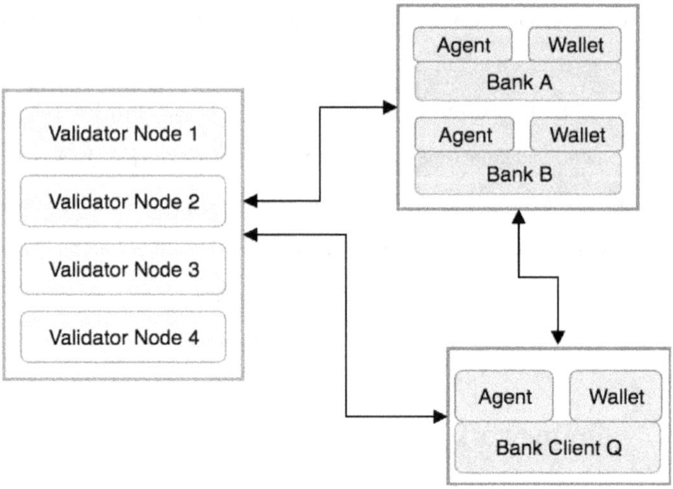

Figure 5.1: Architecture composed of two banks, a client, and four validator nodes

nodes [284]. The banks and the client access the validator nodes through their respective SSI agents. SSI agents are described in Chapter 2.

5.2.2 Simulation

In our KYC2 simulation, there are two banks, A and B, and a client, Q. Client Q is interested in opening an account with a bank. To do so, Q provides bank A with all the necessary identification documents. Bank A verifies Qs identity, opens an account for Q, and issues a Verifiable Credential signed by the bank's private key. This Verifiable Credential is stored securely by Q and can be used to interact with other banks.

Next, client Q decides to open a new account with bank B. Instead of presenting physical identification documents and undergoing the same verification process, Q uses their Verifiable Credential to prove their identity to bank B. Once bank B verifies Qs credentials, it proceeds to open a new account for Q.

The following paragraphs describe the simulation in more detail. Figure 5.2 illustrates the primary interactions in our simulation. The simulation is divided into two phases: *Boot-*

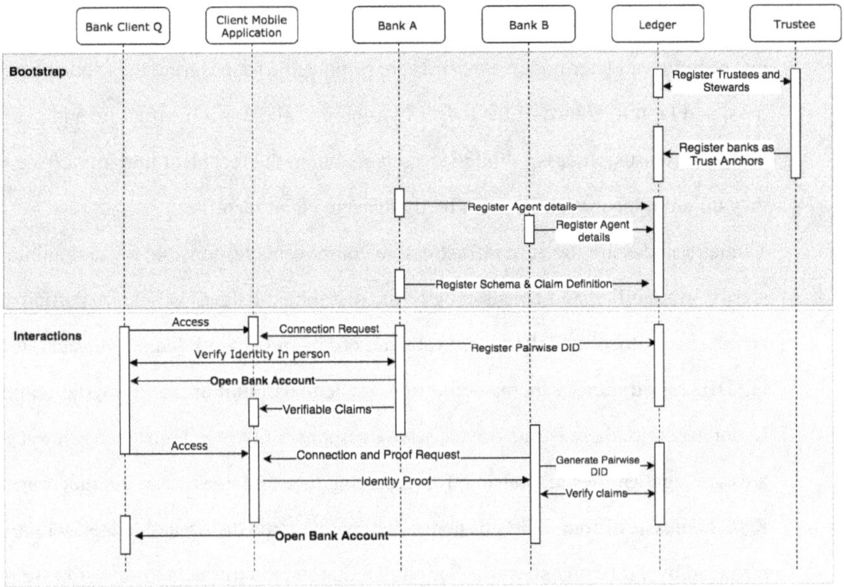

Figure 5.2: Interaction among client, banks and the ledger during bootstrapping and interaction phases

strap (represented by the top area in Figure 5.2) and *Interaction* (depicted by the bottom area in Figure 5.2).

Bootstrap Phase

The bootstrap phase involves registering the necessary data to the ledger, enabling entities to locate, identify, and establish trust with one another. This process begins by adding a trustee and stewards to the ledger.

In Hyperledger Indy, a trustee is a highly privileged governance entity responsible for initializing and overseeing the ledger. The trustee has the authority to assign steward roles and establish the initial trust relationships required for network operation, but does not participate in routine identity issuance or validation activities.

A steward is an authorized organizational entity entrusted with operating and maintaining one or more validator nodes. Stewards are responsible for ensuring the availability, correctness, and fault tolerance of the ledger by running validator infrastructure and participating in the consensus process. While stewards maintain the technical integrity of the network, they do not issue credentials or directly manage client identities.

Validator nodes are the core infrastructure components responsible for maintaining the integrity, availability, and consistency of the distributed ledger. Validators participate in the consensus protocol to collectively validate, order, and commit ledger transactions, including DID registrations, schema definitions, credential definitions, and revocation updates.

In our scenario, there is one trustee whose responsibility is to register the stewards. Stewards are legal entities responsible for managing the validator nodes. As mentioned earlier, KYC2 consists of four validator nodes that maintain the distributed ledger, with each node managed by a different steward. For our simulation, the trustee and stewards are programmatically generated and added to the ledger.

The bootstrap process continues with the addition of banks A and B as trust anchors. The banks must possess a trust anchor role to register the DIDs of their new clients. Figure 5.3 shows an entry within the ledger appointing bank A as a trust anchor. The payload includes several key-value attributes, such as the *dest* attribute, which contains the DID of bank A. Next, the agents communication metadata is broadcasted to the ledger, making them accessible across the network. This metadata includes the agents IP addresses, port numbers, and public keys. The final step of the bootstrap phase involves registering the KYC schema and credential definitions, which are used to issue the Verifiable Credentials. The schema includes the following attributes: *first name, last name, phone number, email,* and *address*. The credential definition includes the public key and revocation details related to bank A. Since A is the only bank in our simulation that issues Verifiable Credentials, it is the sole entity that registers a credential definition with the ledger.

```
[
  {
    "dest": "6qkK4rUpYdNaNTzeDURErE",
    "identifier": "Th7MpTaRZVRYnPiabds81Y",
    "reqId": 1514848463091875,
    "role": "101",
    "signature": "56osaGknV",
    "txnTime": 1514848463,
    "type": "1",
    "verkey": "~ERH3PmtXd2FkuXK7CRwYiw"
  }
]
```

Figure 5.3: Example ledger entry registering a bank as a trust anchor. The bank's DID is stored in the `dest` attribute.

```
{
"connection-request":
  {
    "name": "Bank A",
    "identifier": "6qkK4rUpYdNaNTzeDURErE",
    "nonce": "ousezru20ic4yz3j074trcgthwlsnfsef",
    "endpoint": "10.20.30.105:8888"
  },
  "sig": "oeGeMdt5...fDXAHtLZ9"
}
```

Figure 5.4: Content of the connection-request message sent from bank A to client Q

Interaction Phase

The second phase of the simulation is the interaction phase. This phase begins with client Q accessing their KYC2 wallet to accept a connection request from bank A. This request contains the DID and the necessary connection information required to establish a secure link with the bank. Figure 5.4 shows the content of the connection request received by Q.

Upon acceptance of the request by client Q, they generate a new *pairwise* DID and key pair specific to the communication between A and Q. Bank A is a trust anchor; thus, it can append the new DID and key produced by Q to the ledger. Next, Q presents their identification documentation to A. This is typically a process done in person or through a method supported by the bank. Once Q is fully identified, the bank will open an account for Q and issue a Verifiable Credential through the established secure channel.

Note that client Q can also issue credentials about themselves, but these credentials do not have the same level of trustworthiness and may not be trusted by the banks. Only the banks enrolled in the KYC2 framework are trusted as valid issuers.

At this point, client Q has a Verifiable Credential, which they can use to prove their verified identity with any other bank. Next, Q attempts to open an account with bank B. This begins by Q opening the KYC2 wallet and accepting a connection request from bank B, just as they did with bank A. Figure 5.5 depicts the connection request sent from bank B to Q. As shown in this figure, the request contains a *proof-requests* attribute. The *proof-requests* contains a *name* and *version* attribute, along with the attributes that B expects from Q. The request also contains a *verifiableAttributes* attribute, which holds the list of identity data that will be verified by B.

Since client Q has a Verifiable Credential in their possession, they respond to the connection request with the required Verifiable Credentials (i.e., a presentation derived from the credential). Bank B then verifies the signatures on the credentials and returns a success or failure message to Q. Upon successful identity verification, bank B may proceed with opening an account for Q. Optionally, the details of the consent given by the client, regarding the use of their identity credentials by the banks, are registered on the ledger for future reference and audit.

Going forward, client Q has the ability to register with any other member bank in a similar fashion. As Q interacts with additional banks, they are able to increase their reputation score. A higher score grants Q access to financial services that require higher identity assurance.

5.3 Discussion

This section provides a discussion around decentralized trust and current identity management systems. That is followed by a high-level evaluation of the KYC2 framework against a number of identity principles.

```
{
"connection-request": {
"name": "Bank B",
"identifier": "XFqGpHolgtHgc47BPGsgiS",
"nonce": "57fbf9dc8c8e6ace33de98c6d747b281",
"endpoint": "10.20.30.105:9999"
  },
  "proof-requests": [{
    "name": "KYC-Profile", "version": "0.1",
    "attributes": {
        "first_name": "string", "last_name": "string", "phone_number": "string",
        "email": "string", "address": "string"  },
      "verifiableAttributes": ["first_name", "last_name", "phone_number",
      "address", "email"]
  }],
  "sig": " oeGeMdt5HRjRJZnrpfDXAHtLZ9 "
}
```

Figure 5.5: Content of the connection-request sent from bank B to client Q. This request contains a proof-requests attribute

5.3.1 KYC2 and Decentralized Trust

As mentioned in Chapter 2, Hyperledger Indy relies on distributed ledger technology to provide a decentralized public key infrastructure. Although an exhaustive comparison between PKI-based systems such as PKIX and TLS, with DPKI-based systems such as KYC2 is beyond the scope of this work, it is possible to discuss a number of key points about the two approaches.

One practical challenge in conventional PKI deployments is certificate status management. Mechanisms such as certificate revocation lists (CRLs) and the Online Certificate Status Protocol (OCSP) can introduce operational overhead and, in the case of online status checks, may reveal information about client connections. In contrast, Indy-style ecosystems publish credential definitions and revocation material in a way that supports offline or locally verifiable checks, reducing dependence on issuer availability during verification.

Every KYC2 entity with a trust anchor role is able to register DIDs and cryptographic keys to the ledger. Although this feature places a burden on the trust anchors and the nodes, it allows the formation of an authenticated and encrypted channel between any two entities of the network. While the same process can be implemented on PKI-based protocols such as TLS in the client-server web architecture, it is not common nor the default behavior of the clients to produce and use client-side digital certificates.

While KYC2 has a decentralized architecture, it is nevertheless dependent on trusted sources, such as the government and banks, to perform the initial client identity proofing. Moreover, the current iteration of the KYC2 framework relies on the existence of a supervisory entity with the trustee role, which possesses absolute control over the network. The KYC2 framework requires the development of a *trust framework* that describes the decentralized governance policies and processes by which all entities are enrolled into the KYC2 ecosystem.

A production KYC2 deployment requires a formal trust framework governing:

a) **Governance Structure**

- Steering committee composition (banks, regulators, technology providers)
- Decision-making processes (consensus, voting thresholds)
- Dispute resolution mechanisms

b) **Participation Requirements**

- Credential issuer vetting (financial institution licensing, audit requirements)
- Trust anchor criteria (capital requirements, security certifications)
- Validator node operator qualifications

c) **Technical Standards**

- Credential schema versioning and evolution
- Cryptographic algorithm suites (key sizes, hash functions)
- Revocation update frequency and caching policies

d) **Legal and Compliance**

- Liability allocation (issuer vs verifier responsibilities)
- Cross-jurisdictional recognition (international credential acceptance)
- Regulatory reporting requirements (AML/KYC audit trails)

e) **Operational Policies**

- Incident response procedures (e.g., compromised issuer keys, governance disputes, ledger outages)
- Credential lifecycle management (issuance, renewal, revocation)
- User support and recourse mechanisms

Reference Models: Similar frameworks exist in other SSI ecosystems:

- Sovrin Governance Framework (for general-purpose SSI) [100]
- Verifiable Credentials for Education (for academic credentials) [285]
- GLEIF vLEI (for legal entity identifiers) [286]

KYC2 can adapt these models to the specific requirements of financial services by incorporating regulatory compliance, institutional trust structures, and auditability. Unlike general-purpose SSI ecosystems, financial applications require clearly defined governance, liability boundaries, and cross-jurisdictional recognition to ensure that issued credentials are both technically verifiable and legally accepted.

Finally, the incentive for deployment and operation of KYC2 nodes is an important consideration. Operating validator infrastructure involves non-trivial costs related to security, availability, and compliance. A practical approach is to distribute this responsibility among participating financial institutions in a consortium model, where the benefits include reduced onboarding costs, faster client acquisition, and improved data quality. Incentivizing banks to perform the initial KYC verification is equally critical. Institutions that issue credentials benefit from reduced redundancy in future onboarding and faster service delivery.

Additionally, a fee-sharing model can be introduced, where institutions relying on previously issued credentials compensate the original issuer. This distributes the cost of identity verification across the ecosystem and encourages participation.

5.3.2 Evaluation of KYC2 against Various Identity Principles

In this section, we assess the KYC2 framework against a number of identity and privacy criteria. In order for the KYC2 framework to successfully implement an SSI model, it must address the SSI principles. Table 5.1 maps each SSI principle to a specific requirement of the framework.

GDPR and other new legal frameworks have expedited the need to improve the status quo identity management models. Given that GDPR consists of 11 chapters, 99 articles, and 173 recitals, it is not a minor adaptation. Data controllers and data processors (jointly called data consumers in this section) are subject to GDPR regulations. In the context of KYC2, data consumers include banks, agents, wallets, and ledger nodes. Table 5.2 lists the key principles within Article 5 of GDPR that are related to personal data and their corresponding KYC2 requirements.

Privacy by Design (PbD) is a holistic approach that takes privacy into consideration at every step of the engineering process. To evaluate the KYC2 framework against PbD, Table 5.3 maps each of the seven foundational principles of PbD, as defined by Ann Cavoukian, to the appropriate KYC2 requirement.

5.3.3 Conclusion

Know Your Customer is a resource-intensive and complex process. This chapter described a digital client onboarding system based on Hyperledger Indy and the principles of SSI. Through this work, we aimed to address several key challenges.

First, current identity management models do not always consider users as principal stakeholders. Second, users digital identities are often fragmented across multiple identity

SSI Principles	KYC2 Requirements
Existence	The existence of a real-world identity is verified during the initial interaction between the client and the bank.
Access	All identity attributes and keys are accessible by the client through their wallet. The ledger should be available to the client (optionally through agents) to resolve DIDs to DDOs and obtain public keys and other public data.
Transparency	The KYC2 framework is an open-source project operating on a public permissioned distributed ledger. No personal identity attributes are written to the ledger. Key revocation information, consent receipts, and schemas are all accessible through the ledger. An onboarding process must exist for any entity requiring write access.
Persistence	The DID of each entity, along with agent metadata, consent receipts, and public credentials, is recorded on the ledgermaking them permanent and valid until explicitly invalidated by their owners.
Portability	Client identity data is portable through smartphones, or optionally stored in cloud-based solutions chosen by the client.
Interoperability	KYC2 relies on open data structures and standards such as DIDs and Verifiable Credentials to ensure interoperability among all parties. Standard communication protocols further enhance ecosystem compatibility.
Consent	Clients must explicitly define the terms and policies governing how their attributes are shared with banks. A privacy-preserving consent receipt should be written to the ledger using data-minimization and, where applicable, privacy-enhancing techniques such as selective disclosure and zero-knowledge proofs.
Minimization	Only the attributes specifically required for a bank's regulatory KYC obligations are requested. Zero-knowledge proofs allow the client to further minimize the data disclosed.
Protection	The policies and responsibilities of every entity in the framework must be clearly defined in the KYC2 trust framework. Validator nodes should be geographically distributed, and no single node should be capable of censoring a valid transaction.

Table 5.1: KYC2 Framework and SSI Principles

GDPR Principles	KYC2 Requirements
Data to be processed in a lawful, fair and transparent way	Every KYC2 data consumer must clearly articulate their data processing practices to clients and obtain explicit permission before processing personally identifiable information. Both the client and the involved data consumers should generate a privacy-preserving consent receipt that references their usage agreements. Consent receipts may also document interactions among data consumers. The structure of the consents recorded on the ledger should be well-defined to ensure authorized entities can interpret them correctly.
Purpose limitation	Data consumers should obtain and process only the identity attributes necessary for their operations. For example, agents may require only the clients public keys and decentralized identifiers to establish secure channels with other agents.Banks, by contrast, require identity data sufficient to satisfy Know Your Customer and Anti-Money Laundering regulations.
Data minimization	Only relevant and necessary data should be shared with data consumers, and only for the minimum required duration. Clients should be able to make granular selections of their identity attributes and employ privacy-enhancing techniques such as zero-knowledge proofs.
Accuracy	Clients must be able to update their identification recordssuch as cryptographic keys and decentralized identifiersstored on the ledger and with banks. Banks issuing credentials must ensure the accuracy and integrity of identity verification and credential issuance procedures.
Storage limitation	Although banks have regulatory obligations to retain client data, retention should not exceed what is required by applicable policies. Under Article 17 (Right to be Forgotten), clients may request the deletion of their data. To support this right, no personally identifiable information should ever be written to the ledger. However, immutable data such as DIDs, DDOs, and consent receipts cannot be removed once recorded, though their association with an identifiable subject can be effectively revoked or rendered inactive. Identity data stored by banks, agents, or wallets must be removed promptly upon a clients request, with delays communicated transparently.
Integrity and confidentiality	Data consumers must enforce strong security measures, including proper storage and transmission protections for personal data. Using the public keys and DIDs stored on the ledger, clients and banks can establish secure bidirectional channels. Wallet and agent security require special attention, as these components hold and process sensitive identity information.
Accountability	Data consumers must implement appropriate technical and organizational controls, including accurate record-keeping and incident management. In the event of a data breach, affected entities must promptly notify regulators and impacted clients. Every organization consuming identity data should appoint a data protection officer responsible for ensuring compliance with current and emerging GDPR regulations. Because the KYC2 ecosystem spans diverse entities and jurisdictions, determining responsibility and identifying applicable regulations may be complex, especially during a GDPR-related incident.

Table 5.2: SSI Framework and GDPR Principles

PbD Principles	KYC2 Requirements
Proactive not Reactive, Preventative not Remedial	All entities within the KYC2 ecosystem must commit to strong and proactive privacy and security controls. These commitments should be embedded in the KYC2 trust framework to foster a culture of continuous privacy protection.
Privacy as the Default Setting	By default, only the minimum necessary data should be collected from clients. Privacy-preserving mechanismssuch as zero-knowledge proofs, anonymization, and strong cryptographymust be enabled by default. To maximize network anonymity, a new pairwise DID should be created for each clientbank connection. Banks may choose either a pairwise DID per client or a publicly known persistent DID.
Privacy Embedded into Design	The Hyperledger Indy architecture includes built-in privacy controls such as selective disclosure and zero-knowledge proofs.
Full Functionality, Positive-Sum, not Zero-Sum	Privacy protections should complement, not hinder, system functionality. The ledger should record only public datapublic keys, schemas, credential definitions, and revocation materialwhile still enabling full verification of signatures and credentials. The architecture must prevent issuers from being involved in signature validation queries, and DIDs/signatures must be structured to avoid identity correlation. Although SSI enables clients to control their identity data locally, strong security controls must protect stored identity data and cryptographic keys.
End-to-End Security	Security protections must apply continuouslyfrom issuance of credentials by a bank, to their use as proof by a client, through revocation. These protections must cover data in transit and at rest across wallets, agents, banks, and the ledger.
Visibility and Transparency Keep it Open	The framework is open-source and built on open standards. Entities must agree to the KYC2 trust framework and undergo verification before joining. Clients may choose their preferred agents and wallet implementations. All entities must be open to audit and independent verification.
Respect for User Privacy Keep it User-Centric	KYC2 follows self-sovereign identity principles, ensuring clients maintain full control of their identity data. Client-facing interfaces such as mobile apps, wallets, and agents must be intuitive, user-centric, and privacy-preserving. Clients should be promptly notified of any access to their data.

Table 5.3: KYC2 Framework and Privacy by Design Principles

providers, some of which fail to adhere to industry best practices and privacy standards. This issue is evident in the increasing number of cyberattacks and identity breaches. Furthermore, the introduction of regulations such as the General Data Protection Regulation imposes new perspectives on digital identity rights. This chapter takes a step toward empowering online users in the ongoing effort to protect their digital identities and introduces a novel digital approach to the KYC process.

Chapter 6

Authentic Non-Fungible Tokens Based on a Self-Sovereign Identity Model

6.1 Introduction

Non-fungible tokens (NFTs) have become a major topic in recent years, gaining significant attention since 2021. Despite experiencing cycles of hype and decline, they have contributed to the overall growth of Web3. NFTs represent an interesting application of cryptocurrencies and smart contracts. Many artists, celebrities, and billionaires have become intrigued by the potential of NFTs, helping to introduce them to first-time crypto investors and explorers. In recent years, we have seen continuous growth in NFT collections and applications. In fact, the popularity of the term "NFT" increased by 11,000% in 2021, and the term "NFT" was chosen as Collins Dictionary's Word of the Year [287].

An NFT is a special type of cryptographic token that represents a unique entity. Non-fungible tokens are individually unique and not mutually interchangeable. An NFT is generated by a smart contract, and the contract code is stored on the blockchain. Ethereum was the first blockchain to standardize this type of token into an interface called ERC-721.

While ERC-721 introduces the concept of non-fungible tokens, it does not prescribe all production implementation details. In practice, many requirements such as minting and burning policies, contract-level access control, royalties, and marketplace integration are implemented through additional contract logic and related standards beyond the minimal ERC-721 interface [288]. These capabilities must be developed and integrated by developers.

While NFTs continue to gain cultural relevance, there is also a growing number of threats surrounding their use. This highlights the need for investment in designing robust digital identity and verification protocols to ensure the legitimacy, scarcity, and ownership information of each NFT. NFTs are only as secure as the platforms and protocols on which they run, both of which are susceptible to breaches, hacks, and misuse.

In this chapter, we propose a model based on SSI principles to add a layer of identity management to the generation and exchange of NFTs. Through our model, we enhance assurance about the identity of NFT creators and sellers, enabling buyers and marketplaces to make better-informed trust decisions while preserving user privacy.

6.1.1 Token Standards

Ethereum standards such as ERC-20, ERC-721, and ERC-1155 are specified through the Ethereum Improvement Proposal (EIP) process [289].

ERC-20 represents a standard token interface [290]. It defines a collection of rules that specific entities must follow to ensure interoperability and compatibility with exchanges and wallets operating within the Ethereum ecosystem. As of January 2021, the Ethereum network hosts over 350,000 tokens based on the ERC-20 token standard.

In comparison, ERC-721 defines a single distinct non-fungible asset, which cannot be exchanged on a one-to-one basis. This token standard provides a means of asset tokenization where the asset is indivisible. Every token based on ERC-721 holds information required for ownership tracking and metadata resolution for that particular asset.

In contrast to ERC-20, ERC-721 supports a mapping of a *token ID* to its owner. Through this mapping, each token has its own owner. By comparison, ERC-20 tokens only have a mapping of an address to a balance. Similar to ERC-20 tokens, NFTs can be transferred from one owner to another.

ERC-1155 is another important token standard [291]. This standard forms the foundation

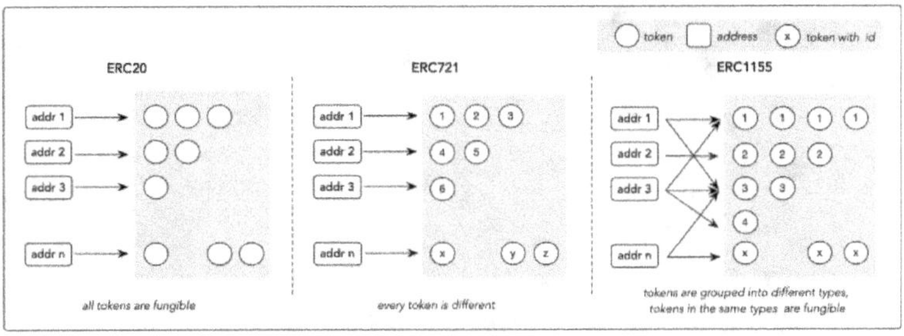

Figure 6.1: NFT Token Standards ERC20, ERC721 and ERC1155

for many NFT use cases. As a superset of ERC-721 functionality, ERC-1155 supports semi-fungibility. Unlike ERC-721, where a unique ID represents a single asset, the unique ID of an ERC-1155 token represents a class of assets. The token includes an additional quantity field to represent the amount of a particular class that an NFT wallet holds. Assets within the same class are interchangeable, and it is possible to transfer any amount of assets to other users. Figure 6.1, sourced from [292], compares the three token types.

Another major difference is the NFT's metadata. Storing data on the blockchain can become significantly expensive. Therefore, as a solution, most NFTs implement a method to store metadata in JSON format by assigning a unique token URI for every token ID [288]. A token URI is an identifier pointing to the media represented by an NFT. The token URI can take any form of URI that points to the metadata. The following Figure 6.2 depicts the link between an NFT marketplace, the ERC721 smart contract, and the storage of ERC721 metadata and assets.

Considering a popular NFT such as 'Bored Ape Yacht Club' an example of a token URI for that NFT collection is "ipfs://QmeSjSinHpPnmXmspMjwiXyN6zS4E9zccariGR3jxcaWtq/1552". The given IPFS URL [74] which resolves to an ERC721 metadata hosted on IPFS as shown in Figure 6.3

In the above example, the image field itself is an IPFS link pointing to an image. In many deployments, the token URI is set at mint time and treated as stable; however, whether it

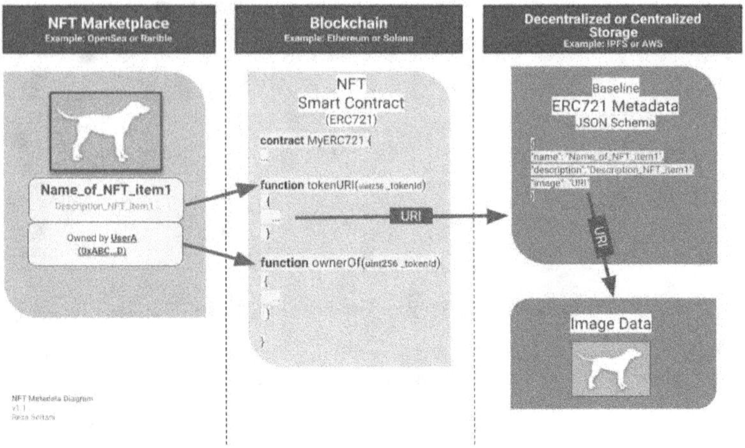

Figure 6.2: ERC721 Data Mapping and Metadata

```
{
  "image": "ipfs://QmahdEypXXrFvBzHEuzt3HmZHeZtUlsPGR85jfeakYc1Wc",
  "attributes": [
    {"trait_type": "Background", "value": "Yellow"},
    {"trait_type": "Eyes", "value": "Eyepatch"},
    {"trait_type": "Fur", "value": "Black"},
    {"trait_type": "Mouth", "value": "Bored Unshaven Cigarette"},
    {"trait_type": "Earring", "value": "Gold Hoop"},
    {"trait_type": "Hat", "value": "Cowboy Hat"}
  ]
}
```

Figure 6.3: Sample NFT metadata of Bored Ape Yacht Club with ID 1552

can be changed depends on the contract design. The token asset metadata are typically hosted on a separate platform, and depending on the storage backend, the metadata may or may not be immutable. It's important to note that the asset metadata is not always hosted on a decentralized storage platform such as IPFS. In many cases, JSON metadata and the NFT asset itself are hosted on the owner's own web server or on a cloud platform such as Amazon Web Services (AWS).

6.1.2 Token Use Cases

ERC-721 NFT tokens have found applications across many domains in the Ethereum space, including gaming, the Metaverse, collectibles, and utilities. In gaming, items can be represented as NFTs, where each item has a unique set of properties and potentially serves as an in-game customization, a power-up, or any other utility. Metaverses are digital environments that provide users and organizations with numerous opportunities to port real-world assets and services while offering an open economy backed by blockchain. NFTs can be integrated into the Metaverse as a way to provide community and social experiences, as well as identity for its users. Many examples of identity-shaping NFTs are used as avatars by users in the Metaverse. These avatars grant their holders exclusive rights and access to certain closed communities and offline private events, bridging the digital and real worlds. NFTs can also support the use, trade, and rental of real estate in the digital world. Collectibles are another great fit for NFTs due to their uniqueness. Lastly, NFTs can enable their owners to gain access to various resources that would otherwise be unavailable, such as limited early access to future products or events.

6.1.3 Scam and Security Challenges

While recent years have seen rapid development, adoption, and sales of NFTs, we have also witnessed a number of setbacks caused by NFT fraud and scams.

These include artist and social media impersonation, fake airdropping and bidding, fake and replica NFT stores [293], as well as scamming users into investing in NFT projects that never existed [294].

Registration of suspicious domains that resemble NFT stores, such as Rarible and OpenSea, has increased in recent years, and there are many instances where hackers try to pass off an artist's work as their own. For example, a fake Banksy NFT linked to Banksy's website was posted and traded on OpenSea's marketplace, where it was sold for nearly 100 Ethereum, worth around $336,000 at the time of sale [295].

New technologies such as NFTs present potential money laundering challenges. While gallerists have incentives to increase awareness and traffic about the artists they represent, and to maintain the reputation of the gallery, sellers of NFTs do not necessarily have the same goals [296].

Moreover, due to the revenue generation model of NFTs, where artists are paid a royalty each time their work is sold, there is an incentive to transact with as many purchasers as possible, with limited interest in the verification of the identity of the buyers of the work. Lack of due diligence and identity verification can potentially lead to money laundering vulnerabilities. Self-laundering occurs when criminals purchase an NFT with illicit funds and continue to transact with themselves to create records of sales [296]. Lack of consistency in identity management and verification among NFT platforms exacerbates money laundering challenges.

In addition, NFTs are susceptible to a particular form of Sybil attack, where one can create multiple accounts on an NFT platform and purchase a particular NFT to artificially drive up its price.

It's important to realize that while some NFT marketplaces have stepped up their verification process recently, there have been instances where hackers were able to complete the verification process to impersonate legitimate creators [297]. Moreover, on most NFT platforms, the publisher does not have to verify that they own the creative work before submitting the NFT to the site and blockchain. Rather, the expectation is for the buyers of NFTs to do their due diligence to ensure they are purchasing NFTs from authentic creators, while at the same time, the creators must check the NFT stores to make sure their works are not published without their consent.

As another key point, in the art industry, investigating the authenticity of art pieces is highly recommended for buyers prior to making a purchase. Buyers must perform extensive due diligence with the help of available tools and services, and investigate the history of ownership and provenance. The details about previous owners should be documented. The NFT space reflects the same issue and measures.

Equally important, there is no global registry of verified NFT issuers, and every NFT store performs its own method of identity verification. For example, Rarible expects a profile image, a cover image, and a bio from creators who wish to verify their account [298]. Rarible also requires a link to a social media account such as Twitter to increase the chance of verification. Finally, at least one item must be minted by the creator to be eligible for the verification process. Creators who are not verified on Rarible do not have their work available on the platform's search results or explore page. Once Rarible receives a verification request, it uses automated scripts and manual evaluation to make sure the requirements mentioned above are met. The verification process also involves Rarible performing a reverse search on the items already posted by the creator on the platform. OpenSea has a similar verification process [299]. Users who wish to have their account verified must have a valid profile and cover image, an email address, and be active on the platform. Next, the accounts must belong to one of four categories: well-known individuals or organizations, accounts with unusual fraud risk, accounts with unusual innovations, or accounts verified by valid social media accounts.

It is evident that the introduction of an interoperable and scalable digital identity layer is a critical step toward establishing trust and authenticity in this space, reducing fraud and business risk, and increasing user adoption of the NFT space.

6.1.4 Our Contribution

NFTs are considered beneficial in a wide variety of use cases. Their ability to provide a standardized method of originality and scarcity of information based on cryptography on a decentralized platform is extremely valuable. That being said, as the current design of NFT platforms and recent incidents show, the NFT space suffers from inadequate identity management. The process of establishing identity is the first step in preventing fraud and creating a safe marketplace.

In this chapter, we propose a digital identity layer based on the self-sovereign identity model to address the lack of trust in users' true identity in the NFT space. Our model relies on SSI standards and specifications to design an identity network where users can generate DIDs anchored to an Indy-based ledger. Participants who complete a successful interaction (e.g., a buyer who verifies a seller) may optionally issue a verifiable trust stamp to the counterparty. These trust stamps are implemented as peer-issued verifiable credentials representing individual attestations, and can be presented by sellers as portable reputation signals across future interactions.

These digital stamps provide users with a method to establish credibility and interaction history in the market. Purchasers of NFTs who engage with creators can rely on issuer-signed credentials to verify creator identity, and may additionally use peer-issued trust stamps as portable reputation signals across future interactions.

This chapter contributes a concrete, end-to-end SSI-enabled interaction model for NFT marketplaces, together with a working prototype and performance evaluation.

6.2 Proposed Model

The proposed model is based on a typical scenario of exchanging an NFT between a buyer and a seller. The following subsections describe the main actors, the assumptions, and the model execution in detail.

6.2.1 Actors

Our model consists of three main actors. The first is the seller, an entity who intends to sell an NFT. The second actor is the buyer, who is interested in purchasing an NFT, and the third actor is a trusted authority, such as an NFT marketplace, trusted by all parties. In addition, the model relies on an identity ledger as supporting infrastructure for DID resolution and verifiable credential primitives.

The goal of the seller is to sell their NFT to an interested buyer through a secure and trusted communication channel. The seller may wish to offer optional services or products as part of the NFT transaction.

The objective of the buyer is to verify the seller's identity, optionally purchase the NFT, and establish a secure channel with the seller to exchange additional information.

6.2.2 Major Steps of the Model

As depicted in Figure 6.4, the proposed model is divided into five phases, each corresponding to a distinct interaction boundary among the seller, buyer, marketplace, and the identity infrastructure.

Phase 1: Identity Material Generation and DID Publication

In the initial phase, the seller and buyer generate blockchain wallet addresses for marketplace interactions on Ethereum, and all parties (seller, buyer, and marketplace) generate cryptographic keys for SSI-based authentication and secure messaging. In addition, each party establishes a DID to serve as a persistent identity anchor within the SSI layer.

The seller and marketplace publish the necessary DID resolution data to the identity ledger, including public verification keys and service endpoints required for secure communication. In our prototype, this step is implemented using Indy-style DIDs anchored to a Hyperledger Indy ledger, where DID resolution yields public keys and service endpoints used for DIDComm-based interactions. While this differs from W3C DID method representations, the resolved identity data fulfills the same functional role by enabling discovery of cryptographic material and communication endpoints. Optionally, the sellers published identity information may reference publicly verifiable online presence, such as websites or social media accounts, to support downstream validation.

Phase 2: Marketplace Verification and Credential Issuance

To prevent fraud at the earliest possible stage, identity verification is performed prior to NFT minting or marketplace listing. In this phase, the seller initiates an onboarding and verification process with the NFT marketplace (or an accredited identity provider acting on its behalf).

The marketplace verifies the sellers identity and associated online presence using its internal procedures. Upon successful verification, the marketplace issues an issuer-signed verifiable credential to the seller, binding the verified claims to the sellers DID. The seller retrieves and stores this credential in their wallet. Only after obtaining this issuer-verified credential does the seller proceed to publish an NFT listing on the marketplace. This SSI-gated onboarding mechanism enables preventative fraud control and significantly reduces impersonation, Sybil attacks, and the publication of counterfeit NFTs.

Phase 3: NFT Discovery

In this phase, the buyer searches the NFT marketplace and locates the NFT of interest. The marketplace hosts the NFT listing and associated metadata, including the sellers public profile. As part of this profile, the sellers DID is made available to enable identity verification in subsequent phases. At this stage, no direct interaction occurs between the buyer and seller beyond asset discovery.

Phase 4: DID Resolution and Secure Communication Establishment

After identifying an NFT of interest, the buyer extracts the sellers DID from the marketplace profile and resolves it using the identity ledger. Through this resolution process, the buyer obtains the sellers public keys and service endpoints required to establish a secure communication channel.

Using these endpoints, the buyer and seller establish a secure peer-to-peer channel (e.g., via DIDComm) to enable authenticated and confidential communication. At this stage, the buyer may optionally perform preliminary validation of the sellers publicly referenced online presence, such as verifying consistency between claimed domains or social media accounts and the sellers published identity information. This step provides early risk reduction prior to requesting stronger cryptographic proof.

Phase 5: Verifiable Proof, Transaction, and Reputation Update

In the final phase, the buyer requests cryptographic proof from the seller in the form of a verifiable presentation. The seller generates a verifiable presentation in response to the buyers proof request using previously issued issuer-signed credentials, applying selective disclosure and predicate proofs as needed to minimize data exposure.

The buyer verifies the verifiable presentation, validating the credential issuer, integrity, and requested claims. If the buyer is satisfied with the proof, the buyer proceeds to purchase the NFT through the marketplace, and the marketplace updates the NFT listing and ownership state accordingly.

Optionally, following successful verification and transaction completion, the buyer may issue a new verifiable credential to the seller as a verification point or trust stamp. This buyer-issued credential represents successful interaction history and can be retained by the seller for use in future marketplace interactions, contributing to a decentralized and portable reputation mechanism.

6.3 Prototype Development

The implementation of this model consists of two main steps. In the first step, we publish a sample NFT to an NFT marketplace. In the second step, we implement our SSI model to execute the phases described above.

6.3.1 Launch of a Test NFT

We mint an NFT on the OpenSea NFT marketplace [300]. Minting an NFT refers to the process of converting digital files into digital assets backed by the blockchain. OpenSea is a widely used NFT marketplace. Our sample NFT is minted using the ERC-1155 token standard and is a JPEG image shown in Figure 6.5. Although ERC-721 is used throughout this chapter to explain NFT metadata and token URI conventions, the proposed SSI identity layer is token-standard agnostic and applies equally to ERC-721 and ERC-1155 marketplace listings.

The Table 6.1 shows the contract address, token ID, and the transaction associated with the submission.

The process of deploying an NFT to OpenSea is as follows. Initially, we purchased a certain amount of Ethereum cryptocurrency to support the fee associated with blockchain transactions. Next, we created an Ethereum wallet to hold our Ethereum funds and to buy or sell NFTs. The MetaMask browser extension is a popular crypto wallet that is fully supported by OpenSea [301]. We then connected our wallet to the OpenSea platform and created our OpenSea account. Afterward, we created a new collection and uploaded the digital image. We then filled in the properties and descriptions of the NFT. Finally, we selected "Create" to mint the NFT and executed the necessary Ethereum contract. After this stage, our test NFT is published to OpenSea and referenced on the Ethereum blockchain.

Name	To the Moon and Beyond
Collection's Name	To The Moon and Beyond!
Contract's Address	`0x495f947276749ce646f68ac8c248420045cb7b5e`
Token ID	`88319289115386724837938726901891922875` `021916891326102510059840263573148270593`
Token Standard	ERC-1155
Blockchain	Ethereum

Table 6.1: NFT metadata for the asset *To the Moon and Beyond*

6.3.2 SSI Implementation

We begin this section by listing the requirements of our digital wallet in order to support our goals. There are 8 main requirements, namely:

- Interface with a blockchain network as an anchor to store credential schemas and DIDs
- Generate new cryptographic keys and DIDs
- Issue verifiable credentials
- Issue proof requests
- Generate verifiable presentations in response to a proof request
- Establish a secure communication channel between agents
- Validate verifiable presentations
- Exchange secure messages between agents

Actors and Trust Model

Our prototype implementation addresses three distinct roles. The first actor is an issuer of VCs. Any entity in the network, including a well-known marketplace organization, a financial institution, a telecommunication company, or a government entity, can be assigned the authority to issue credentials. In our example, the issuer is a reputable and trusted NFT marketplace capable of performing a thorough identity verification against the seller.

The second actor in the prototype is the seller of an NFT who engages with the issuer through an identity verification process to obtain verifiable credentials.

Finally, the third actor is the buyer of the NFT, who engages with the seller to verify their identity by requesting a verifiable presentation from them and then executing a purchase transaction upon satisfactory identity verification.

The issuer is a trusted entity in the ecosystem, trusted by both the seller and the buyer. Applying the model described in Figure 6.4, a buyer is a VC holder, an issuer, and a verifier, while a seller is a VC holder. The NFT marketplace is a holder and an issuer of VCs.

Deployment Architecture

Our proposed architecture consists of three layers: the ledger, the agents, and the controller.

Ledger Layer

The ledger layer is developed using Hyperledger Indy, a distributed ledger specifically designed for decentralized identity use cases. Indy has native support for DID-related ledger objects and AnonCreds primitives, including schemas, credential definitions, and revocation registries. However, operations to produce and transfer NFTs in our example rely on the Ethereum blockchain. No cross-chain bridge is required in this design: Ethereum maintains NFT ownership and transfer state, while Indy maintains identity and credential state. The application layer (i.e., the marketplace profile and DIDComm interactions) binds an Ethereum account to a seller DID by requiring the seller to present issuer-signed credentials associated with the DID, which buyers can later verify when evaluating a listing.

Although it's possible to use an existing Indy ledger, we deploy a local ledger to have full control over its capabilities and performance. To this end, we run a local version of the Indy network designed by the Verifiable Organization Network (VON) [302]. To launch the network, we deploy four Docker instances of Indy server nodes and another instance for the Indy web interface. The web interface can be accessed through the local URL address "http://localhost:9000".

Any agent that needs to connect to the ledger requires a genesis file. A genesis file contains the necessary information for an agent to locate and establish secure communication with the Indy nodes. Figure 6.6 is an excerpt from the genesis file that describes the access URL, port number, and other details of one of the four nodes.

Agent Layer

Agents are responsible for data storage, message exchange, and protocol state management. Our agent layer is built on the Hyperledger Aries Cloud Agent Python (ACA-Py) architecture. ACA-Py provides a RESTful API interface for administering the agent's internal state and generating communication with other agents. Internally, ACA-Py relies on a PostgreSQL database and Docker engine. ACA-Py supports Hyperledger Indy AnonCreds [303] verifiable credentials, and the W3C Standard Verifiable Credential formats using JSON-LD with support for both LD-Signatures [72] and BBS+ Signatures [304]. For reproducibility, our prototype uses ACA-Py v0.7.4. Figure 6.7, obtained from Hyperledger, depicts the ACA-Py architecture.

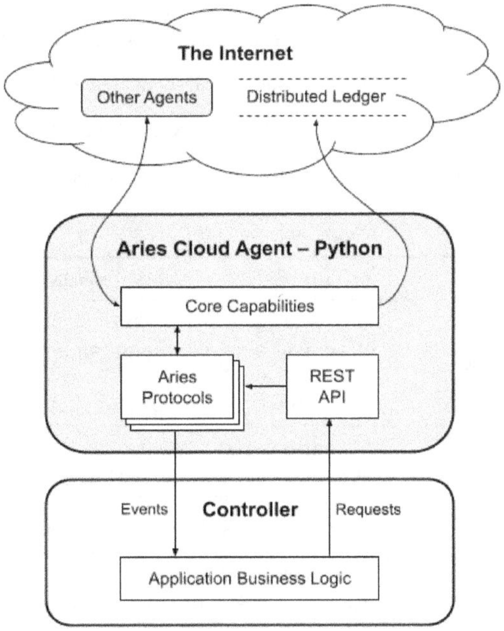

Figure 6.7: Hyperledger Aries Cloud Agent Python (ACA-Py) Architecture

Controller Layer

The controller layer consists of the business logic and the user-facing application layer that relies on the API endpoints provided by ACA-Py. This layer implements the user flow to allow for the execution of the necessary operations, such as credential issuance, connection requests, proof requests, and claim verification.

6.3.3 Program Execution

In this section, we describe a concrete execution of the five phases shown in Figure 6.4. The following scenario is based on a routine interaction among a seller, a buyer, and a marketplace.

Wallet Creation and DID Publication

The first step consists of generating and registering the DIDs of the marketplace, the seller, and the buyer on the ledger. Registering a DID publishes DID resolution data (e.g., verification keys and communication endpoints) required for authentication and secure message exchange. Table 6.2 displays the seed value, public keys, and DIDs of the aforementioned three actors.

Actor	**Details**	
Marketplace	**Seed**	`d_000000000000000000000000941837`
	Public key	`8rPtShxFconRUR5qNRXpBWdWxjdSjvQ2DDFWfkGgez6V`
	DID	`FQXzSr4SaoPUiW2iVs65hC`
Seller	**Seed**	`000000000000000000000000000000BB`
	Public key	`6QjseoubDik4CG2WmRr7nmY8xPtD15ewSgMiGF6zx9sk`
	DID	`AvdgDeUKUpqGrK8vQcUcG7`
Buyer	**Seed**	`d_000000000000000000000000219328`
	Public key	`9TgQeHMAXAvncSuEtSoaEyTPB9x47aRUYNkeyoMrH2v`
	DID	`GXGqj4GKqJkapS2t8eYwF`

Table 6.2: Seed value, DID, and public key of the actors involved

Schema Generation

Prior to passing any credentials, we need to create a credential definition. A prerequisite to credential definition is creating a schema. Both the credential definition and the schema are registered on the ledger [209]. A credential definition contains data required for credential issuance as well as credential validation. A credential definition references a Credential Schema. A Credential Schema is a document that is used to provide a structure and semantics to describe a set of claims comprising a Verifiable Credential. A shared Credential Schema allows all parties to reference the credential in the same way. A schema and credential definition are published to the ledger by the issuers of Verifiable Credentials. In our scenario, the marketplace issues the seller verification credential (thus publishing its schema and credential definition), and the buyer issues an optional trust-stamp credential after successful verification (thus publishing a separate schema and credential definition). The following Figure 6.8 shows the credential schema published by the marketplace to the ledger. Similarly, the buyer issues a separate schema to the ledger, as shown in Figure 6.9.

Verifiable Credential Generation and Issuance to Seller

Following the creation of DIDs and credential schemas, the seller engages with the marketplace to obtain a verifiable credential. In order for the seller to connect with the marketplace, they require an invitation. The marketplace publishes its invitation details on its website. The following Figure 6.10 shows the invitation details of the marketplace.

Once the invitation is read by the seller, a response is created and sent back to the marketplace. The following Figure 6.11 shows the response sent from the seller to the marketplace.

Upon receiving the response from the marketplace, a secure communication channel is established between the seller and the marketplace. From here, the marketplace will perform out-of-band identity verification of the seller. Once the verification is successful, the marketplace will issue a verifiable credential to the seller. Given that there is a secure communication channel between the parties, the marketplace may exchange encrypted messages with the seller to obtain additional information required for credential issuance. The VC sent to the seller is shown in Figure 6.12. The issued VC consists of a certified list of claims, which include a timestamp, username, location, name, birth date, and the web address of the seller.

From this point onward, the seller possesses a verifiable credential that can be shared with any interested buyer, seller, or marketplace. Optionally, the seller can add self-attested claims to their wallet. It is up to the consumer of the claims to accept or reject the self-signed claims.

Verifiable Presentation Requested by the Buyer

At this stage, a buyer wishes to learn more about the seller to verify the authenticity of an NFT. To do so, the buyer engages in a process similar to that of the marketplace and the seller. The buyer identifies the seller's DID through their profile on the NFT marketplace. The buyer then resolves the seller's DID to a DID Document to obtain the seller's service endpoints. Next, the buyer sends their invitation details to the seller. Similar to the previous interaction between the seller and the marketplace, the seller accepts the invitation and responds to the buyer. At this point, a secure communication channel is established between the buyer and the seller. Upon reviewing the seller's profile, the buyer decides to request verifiable proof from the seller. The following Figure 6.13 displays the proof request sent from the buyer to the seller. As shown in the figure, the requested fields include name, username, timestamp, and a zero-knowledge predicate verifying that the seller's birthday is over 18.

Verifiable Presentation Validation and Credential Issuance by Buyer

Upon successful validation of the verifiable presentation provided by the seller, the buyer proceeds with the purchase of the NFT. The transfer of the NFT itself is outside the scope of this work. After validating the seller and optionally purchasing the NFT, the buyer may issue a verification point in the form of a verifiable credential to the seller. To do so, the buyer will present a credential offer to the seller. Once the seller accepts the offer, the buyer will issue a credential consisting of the seller's name, username, web address, and date of the transaction. At this stage, the seller can optionally present the credentials issued by the marketplace and buyers of their NFTs in their wallet and online profiles.

6.4 Performance Evaluation

In this section, we evaluate the performance of the proposed ecosystem by benchmarking the credential issuance workflow between an issuer (such as a marketplace) and a holder wallet (such as a seller). The objective of this evaluation is to measure the latency and throughput characteristics of issuer-to-holder verifiable credential issuance under increasing workload, and to assess whether this overhead remains predictable as the number of credentials grows.

The evaluation focuses exclusively on credential issuance operations, including schema publication, credential definition registration, connection establishment, and credential issuance. Verification and proof presentation operations are outside the scope of this performance study and are not included in the reported measurements.

Similar to the model execution described earlier, the evaluation relies on a local deployment of four Hyperledger Indy validator nodes. All agent interactions are executed using ACA-Py.

6.4.1 Benchmark Setup

Our performance script initializes two wallets: an issuer wallet and a holder (seller) wallet. Each benchmark iteration executes the following sequence of operations:

a) The issuer publishes a credential schema to the ledger.

b) The issuer publishes a credential definition associated with the schema.

c) The issuer and holder establish a secure connection using a DID-based handshake.

d) The issuer issues a credential offer to the holder.

e) The issuer issues a verifiable credential to the holder, which the holder accepts and stores.

The experiments were conducted on a MacBook Pro (2021) equipped with an Apple M1 processor and 16 GB of memory. All Indy nodes and agents were deployed locally using Docker containers, and communication among agents occurred over local TCP connections.

6.4.2 Experiment One: Single-Round Issuance Scaling

The first experiment evaluates the cost of issuing multiple credentials sequentially within a single execution round. In this experiment, the issuer and holder exchange an increasing number of credentials in one round of execution. Table 6.3 presents the total execution time, average issuance time per credential, and effective issuance frequency.

Test Num.	Credentials Issued	Rounds of Test	Total Duration	Average Time per Credential	Frequency per Credential
1	1	1	2.29s	2.29s	0.44/s
2	2	1	3.51s	1.75s	0.57/s
3	3	1	4.31s	1.44s	0.70/s
4	4	1	5.16s	1.29s	0.77/s
5	5	1	6.09s	1.22s	0.82/s
6	10	1	11.34s	1.13s	0.88/s
7	100	1	100.38s	1.00s	1.00/s

Table 6.3: Experiment One: Performance evaluation of SSI credential issuance within a single execution round, where each credential is issued sequencially

The results demonstrate near-linear scaling behavior. As the number of credentials increases, the average issuance time per credential converges toward approximately one second. This behavior indicates that credential issuance overhead remains stable and predictable as workload increases, with fixed setup costs amortized over larger credential batches.

6.4.3 Experiment Two: Multi-Round Issuance Stability

The second experiment evaluates issuance stability across repeated execution rounds. In this setup, a fixed number of credentials is issued per round, and each configuration is executed over 10 rounds to assess performance consistency under sustained workloads. The values reported in Table 6.4 represent the number of credentials processed within each individual round. This experimental design enables the analysis of batch-based issuance behavior over time, providing insights into system stability, throughput consistency, and the absence of cumulative performance degradation. Table 6.4 reports the total execution duration, average execution time per round, and round-level throughput.

Test Num.	Credentials per Round	Rounds of Test	Total Duration	Average Time per Round	Frequency per Round
1	10	10	17.08s	1.71s	0.59/s
2	50	10	73.12s	7.31s	0.14/s
3	100	10	150.34s	15.03s	0.07/s
4	500	10	800.1s	80.01s	0.01/s

Table 6.4: Experiment Two: Performance evaluation of SSI credential issuance across 10 execution rounds, where credentials are issued in a batch

The results show that the average execution time per round increases as the number of credentials processed within each round grows, reflecting the additional workload per batch. Despite this increase, the system maintains predictable and stable performance across all configurations, with no significant degradation observed over repeated execution cycles. The linear growth in round duration indicates that the system scales proportionally with batch size, while the consistency across 10 rounds demonstrates reliable behavior under sustained workloads. Together with the findings from Experiment One, these results confirm that the system achieves both scalable credential issuance and stable long-term operation, supporting its practical deployment in real-world SSI environments.

6.4.4 Discussion

Across both experiments, credential issuance operations exhibit predictable and near-linear performance characteristics. Experiment One demonstrates that sequential issuance scales linearly with the number of credentials, while Experiment Two confirms that repeated issuance across many rounds maintains stable execution time.

These results suggest that SSI-based credential issuance, when implemented using Hyperledger Indy and Aries, introduces manageable overhead and can support sustained onboarding and credential distribution workflows without becoming a bottleneck at the issuerholder interaction level. While proof generation and verification performance are not evaluated in this section, the observed issuance characteristics indicate that SSI-based identity onboarding can scale effectively for marketplace and platform-level deployments.

6.4.5 SSI Frameworks and Comparative Analysis

There are a variety of SSI vendors and implementations available in the market. These implementations range from fully open-source solutions to commercial and cloud-based services. Almost all SSI vendors maintain a GitHub repository with varying degrees of implementation for SSI features and requirements. Our criteria for selecting a suitable solution are based on answering the following questions:

a) Does the framework provide adequate support for the generation and management of DID and DID documents?

b) Does the framework provide sufficient support for the creation, transfer, and consumption of verifiable credentials and verifiable presentations?

c) Does the framework support a connector to a decentralized registry to perform DID registration and lookups?

d) Is there adequate community support for deploying, maintaining, and enhancing the framework, and ensuring that the framework is properly patched based on the latest changes to SSI specifications?

The following Table 6.5 and 6.6 provide a comparison of the open-source SSI frameworks we evaluated. In our evaluation, we considered uPort, Sovrin, Lissi, Mattr, Bloom [305], and SelfKey [306].

Sovrin is an SSI network managed by Sovrin nodes and developed based on the Hyperledger Indy blockchain. Sovrin is a decentralized, global public utility for self-sovereign identity, standardizing the online identity format and the verification of those credentials. Polkadot [307] and other interoperability approaches have motivated research and engineering efforts toward cross-chain connectivity, which may enable more streamlined interactions between SSI networks (e.g., Indy-based ecosystems) and Ethereum-based applications.

uPort and related Ethereum-based SSI efforts have explored DID and credential management on Ethereum. For example, ERC-1056 has been used as a DID registry approach on Ethereum, and credential-related registries have been proposed to support discovery and verification workflows.

Civic supports DID and VC management, in addition to identity verification through biometrics and optical character recognition (OCR). Civic provides its own ERC20 token called Civic to support settlements among participants in identity-related transactions within the ecosystem.

Bloom relies on the Bitcoin blockchain. Similar to Civic, Bloom supports an ERC20 token. An important feature of Bloom is its ability to store data in a Merkle tree, with only the root of the tree being stored on the chain.

Various closed-source solutions, such as Nugget, Veres One, and Digital Bazaar, support the principles of SSI. However, being closed-source, they are not suitable for our experiments.

N. Naik and P. Jenkins provide a comparative analysis of the uPort and Sovrin frameworks, identifying various commonalities and differences between the two implementations [308], [309]. Based on the criteria described above and Table ??, we decided to implement our solution based on Hyperledger Indy and Aries, as they provide the most comprehensive and accessible implementation of SSI requirements.

6.5 Conclusion

Non-fungible Tokens are an emerging technology that is rapidly gaining traction in the blockchain and Metaverse spaces. Despite their potential, the NFT and Metaverse ecosystems suffer from fragmented and inconsistent identity verification practices among participating actors.

In this chapter, we proposed an SSI layer for the NFT and Web3 ecosystems, aimed at providing buyers with assurances regarding the identity of sellers. To this end, we discussed the building blocks of self-sovereign identity and demonstrated the process of generating a sample NFT on the OpenSea marketplace. We also described the architecture of our model implementation and illustrated the step-by-step execution of our prototype based on a typical purchase transaction. Finally, we provided a performance evaluation of the model.

Provider	Product	License	Num. of Contributors
Hyperledger	Hyperledger Indy	Apache-2.0	61
ArcBlock	DID Wallet	MIT, Apache-2.0	3
Lissi	Identity Wallet	Closed-source proprietary, based on Hyperledger Aries	N/A
Trinsic	Trinsic SDK, Wallet, Issuer and Verifier	Apache-2.0, based on Hyperledger Aries	13
SelfKey Foundation	SelfKey Wallet	MIT	21
Mattr	Mattr Wallet	Apache-2.0	15
Bloom	Bloom SSI SDK	Apache-2.0	3
Veramo/uPort	Veramo Core and Plugins	Apache-2.0	32

Table 6.5: Self-sovereign identity framework providers, product names, licenses, and contributor counts

Provider	Underlying Network	Language
Hyperledger	Hyperledger Indy	Rust, Go, Java
ArcBlock	Bitcoin, Ethereum, Hyperledger	JavaScript
Lissi	Hyperledger Indy	N/A
Trinsic	Hyperledger	Dart, C#
SelfKey Foundation	Ethereum	JavaScript
Mattr	Hyperledger Indy	N/A
Bloom	Ethereum and IPFS	TypeScript
Veramo/uPort	Ethereum	TypeScript

Table 6.6: Self-sovereign identity framework providers, their underlying networks, and development languages used

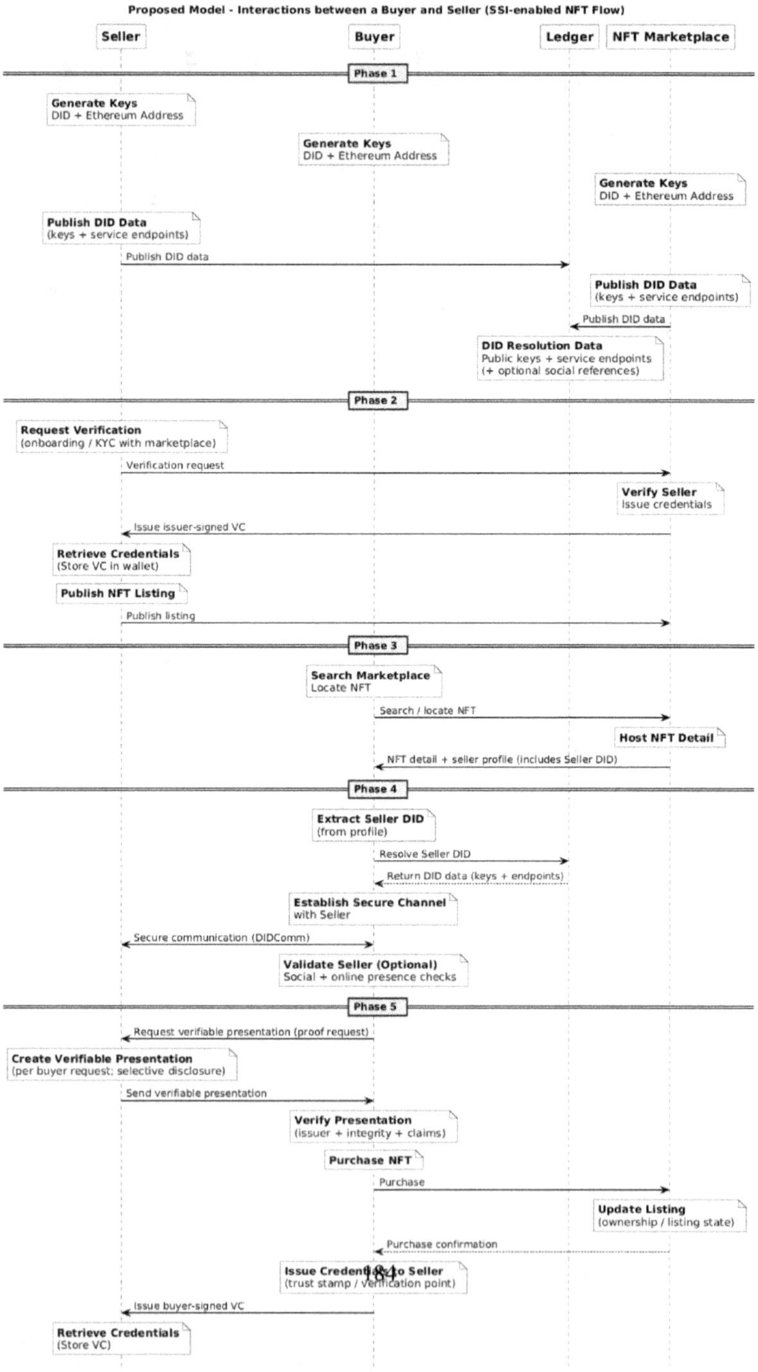
Proposed Model - Interactions between a Buyer and Seller (SSI-enabled NFT Flow)
Seller
Buyer
Ledger
NFT Marketplace
Phase 1
Generate Keys
DID + Ethereum Address
Generate Keys
DID + Ethereum Address
Generate Keys
DID + Ethereum Address
Publish DID Data
(keys + service endpoints)
Publish DID data
Publish DID Data
(keys + service endpoints)
Publish DID data
DID Resolution Data
Public keys + service endpoints
(+ optional social references)
Phase 2
Request Verification
(onboarding / KYC with marketplace)
Verification request
Verify Seller
Issue credentials
Issue issuer-signed VC
Retrieve Credentials
(Store VC in wallet)
Publish NFT Listing
Publish listing
Phase 3
Search Marketplace
Locate NFT
Search / locate NFT
Host NFT Detail
NFT detail + seller profile (includes Seller DID)
Phase 4
Extract Seller DID
(from profile)
Resolve Seller DID
Return DID data (keys + endpoints)
Establish Secure Channel
with Seller
Secure communication (DIDComm)
Validate Seller (Optional)
Social + online presence checks
Phase 5
Request verifiable presentation (proof request)
Create Verifiable Presentation
(per buyer request; selective disclosure)
Send verifiable presentation
Verify Presentation
(issuer + integrity + claims)
Purchase NFT
Purchase
Update Listing
(ownership / listing state)
Purchase confirmation
Issue Credentials to Seller
(trust stamp / verification point)
Issue buyer-signed VC
Retrieve Credentials
(Store VC)

Figure 6.5: Sample NFT deployed to Marketplace


```
{
  "reqSignature": {},
  "txn": {
    "data": {
      "data": {
        "alias": "Node1",
        "blskey": "4N8aUN...LKm3Ba",
        "blskey_pop": "RahHYi...PNdAX1",
        "client_ip": "host.docker.internal",
        "client_port": 9702,
        "node_ip": "host.docker.internal",
        "node_port": 9701,
        "services": [
          "VALIDATOR"
        ]
      },
      "dest": "Gw6...pLhPhv"
    },
    "metadata": {
      "from": "Th7MpTaRZVRYnPiabds81Y"
    },
    "type": "0"
  },
  "txnMetadata": {
    "seqNo": 1,
    "txnId": "fea82e...950b62"
  },
  "ver": "1"
}
```


Figure 6.6: Genesis file describing an Indy node

```
{
  "schema_id": "FQXzSr4SaoPUiW2iVs65hC:2:cert schema:38.82.89",
  "schema": {
    "ver": "1.0",
    "id": "FQXzSr4SaoPUiW2iVs65hC:2:cert schema:38.82.89",
    "name": "cert schema",
    "version": "38.82.89",
    "attrNames": [
      "web",
      "location",
      "username",
      "name",
      "birthdate_dateint",
      "timestamp"
    ],
    "seqNo": 42
  }
}
```


Figure 6.8: Credential schema generated by the marketplace


```
{
  "schema_id": "GXGqj4GKqJkapS2t8eYwF:2:point schema:39.83.91",
  "schema": {
    "ver": "1.0",
    "id": "GXGqj4GKqJkapS2t8eYwF:2:point schema:39.83.91",
    "name": "point schema",
    "version": "39.83.91",
    "attrNames": [
      "web",
      "username",
      "name",
      "date"
    ],
    "seqNo": 48
  }
}
```


Figure 6.9: Credential schema generated by the buyer


```
{
  "@type": "https://didcomm.org/out-of-band/1.1/invitation",
  "@id": "156d1db0-d6b2-4774-a2c3-d879817cf443",
  "handshake_protocols": [
    "https://didcomm.org/didexchange/1.0"
  ],
  "services": [{
    "id": "#inline",
    "type": "did-communication",
    "recipientKeys": ["did:key:z6Mkh8W....4T1RvXGEw"],
    "serviceEndpoint": "http://host.docker.internal:8020"
  }],
  "label": "certifier.agent"
}
```


Figure 6.10: Invitation produced by the marketplace

```
{
  "trace": false,
  "oob_id": "45c08ffe-e92d-4d5d-9e7c-5eb866272513",
  "invi_msg_id": "156d1db0-d6b2-4774-a2c3-d879817cf443",
  "created_at": "2023-01-12T05:07:37.757835Z",
  "state": "deleted",
  "invitation": {
    "@type": "https://didcomm.org/out-of-band/1.1/invitation",
    "@id": "156d1db0-d6b2...a2c3-d879817cf443",
    "services": [
      {
        "id": "#inline",
        "type": "did-communication",
        "recipientKeys": [
          "did:key:z6Mkh....H3PntsEH4T1RvXGEw"
        ],
        "serviceEndpoint": "http://host.docker.internal:8020"
      }
    ],
    "handshake_protocols": [
      "https://didcomm.org/didexchange/1.0"
    ],
    "label": "certifier.agent"
  },
  "connection_id": "50de80a8-3bba-4609...2fdfd9d17bda",
  "role": "receiver",
  "updated_at": "2023-01-12T05:07:37.757835Z"
}
```


Figure 6.11: Invitation response from the seller to the marketplace


```
{
  "referent": "3c50a58b-4c4a-4c51...-7dfaca6ebaf9",
  "schema_id": "FQXzSr4SaoPUiW2iVs65hC:2:cert schema:38.82.89",
  "cred_def_id": "FQXzSr4SaoPUiW2iVs65hC:3:CL:42:certifier.agent.cert_schema",
  "rev_reg_id": null,
  "cred_rev_id": null,
  "attrs": {
    "timestamp": "1673500339",
    "username": "Cosmic_Illustrations",
    "location": "Toronto",
    "name": "Reza Soltani",
    "birthdate_dateint": "19990112",
    "web": "beyondthemoon.info"
  }
}
```


Figure 6.12: Verifiable credential issued by the marketplace to the seller

```
{
  "name": "Proof of Certification",
  "version": "1.0",
  "requested_attributes": {
    "0_name_uuid": {
      "name": "name",
      "restrictions": [{
        "schema_name": "cert schema"
      }]
    },
    "0_username_uuid": {
      "name": "username",
      "restrictions": [{
        "schema_name": "cert schema"
      }]
    },
    "0_timestamp_uuid": {
      "name": "timestamp",
      "restrictions": [{
        "schema_name": "cert schema"
      }]
    }
  },
  "requested_predicates": {
    "0_birthdate_dateint_LE_uuid": {
      "name": "birthdate_dateint",
      "p_type": "<=",
      "p_value": 20050416,
      "restrictions": [{
        "schema_name": "cert schema"
      }]
    }
  }
}
```


Figure 6.13: Verifiable credential proof requested by the buyer from the seller


```
{
  "referent": "8f37fd77-4dfe-...-d21694679659",
  "schema_id": "GXGqj4GKqJkapS2t8eYwF:2:point schema:76.40.10",
  "cred_def_id": "GX....203:buyer.agent.point_schema",
  "rev_reg_id": null,
  "cred_rev_id": null,
  "attrs": {
    "date": "2023-04-16",
    "username": "Cosmic_Illustrations",
    "web": "www.zeroknowledgeproof.com",
    "name": "Reza Soltani"
  }
}
```


Figure 6.14: Verifiable credential provided by the buyer to the seller after a successful verification

Chapter 7

Conclusion and Future Research Directions

This dissertation presented a comprehensive study of the Self-Sovereign Identity model and its potential to transform modern digital identity management systems. The dissertation examined the conceptual foundations of digital identity, the architectural components that enable decentralized identity infrastructures, and the practical challenges associated with deploying SSI in real-world environments. Through this work, we analyzed the evolution of identity management models, identified key limitations in centralized and federated identity systems, and explored how SSI architecturessupported by decentralized identifiers, verifiable credentials, and privacy-preserving cryptographic techniquescan provide a more user-centric and privacy-respecting approach to digital identity.

Beyond surveying the landscape of decentralized identity systems, this dissertation investigated several fundamental research questions that are critical to the design and adoption of SSI architectures. These questions focus on secure key management, privacy-preserving data sharing, and the practical applicability of SSI in contemporary digital ecosystems.

The first research question examined how users can securely manage their cryptographic keys while maintaining usability and privacy. As discussed in Chapter 3, the proposed approach combines decentralized key recovery mechanisms, biometric authentication, and threshold cryptography to provide a resilient key management architecture. This design improves both security and usability by allowing users to recover cryptographic keys without relying on centralized custodians while minimizing the risks associated with key loss.

The second research question explored how users can maintain control over their personal data and enforce access policies governing how their information is shared. In Chapter

4, we demonstrated that the integration of attribute-based encryption, verifiable credentials, and SSI infrastructure enables users to enforce fine-grained access control policies over their data. This approach allows sensitive information to be shared selectively while ensuring that disclosure occurs only under cryptographically verifiable policy constraints.

The third research question evaluated whether SSI has matured sufficiently to support real-world digital identity use cases. Through the analysis presented in Chapters 5 and 6, we examined practical applications of SSI in domains such as financial identity verification and emerging Web 3.0 ecosystems. Our findings indicate that SSI can provide an effective identity verification layer for scenarios such as Know Your Customer processes in financial institutions, as well as decentralized applications and NFT marketplaces.

Taken together, the research presented in this dissertation contributes to the growing body of knowledge surrounding decentralized identity systems. In particular, this work makes three primary contributions. First, it proposes a privacy-preserving key management and recovery architecture that combines decentralized recovery mechanisms with biometric authentication and threshold cryptography. Second, it introduces a user-controlled data sharing framework based on attribute-based encryption and verifiable credentials that enables fine-grained, policy-driven access control over personal data. Third, it evaluates the applicability of SSI architectures in practical deployment scenarios, demonstrating how decentralized identity infrastructures can support emerging financial and Web 3.0 ecosystems.

While these contributions demonstrate the viability and potential advantages of SSI-based identity systems, the field remains in an early stage of development. Several technical, organizational, and regulatory challenges must still be addressed before SSI can achieve widespread adoption. The following section outlines several promising directions for future research.

7.1 Future Directions of Self-Sovereign Identity

The field of Self-Sovereign Identity continues to evolve rapidly. On one hand, the commercialization of SSI platforms and the emergence of new digital identity initiatives are accelerating the adoption of decentralized identity models. On the other hand, ongoing research in cryptographic protocols, distributed systems, and governance frameworks continues to expand the capabilities of SSI architectures.

Although SSI provides a feature set that rivals traditional identity management systems, challenges such as interoperability, regulatory acceptance, governance design, and user adoption remain important barriers. Nevertheless, continued advances in standards, trust frameworks, and privacy-enhancing technologies position SSI as a promising foundation for future digital identity ecosystems. Based on the research conducted in this dissertation, several future research directions can be identified.

- **Key Management and Recovery**

  Wallet usability and key loss remain one of the largest barriers to SSI adoption. Future research can explore alternative secret-sharing algorithms and recovery protocols to further improve the privacy, security, and performance of decentralized key management systems. In addition, comprehensive security evaluations of emerging architecturesincluding threat modeling and formal verificationcan provide deeper insights into the resilience of decentralized key recovery mechanisms.

- **Reputation-Based Trust Frameworks for KYC**

  Another promising direction involves integrating reputation-based scoring models within decentralized KYC ecosystems. Such systems could allow clients to build trust scores as they interact with multiple financial institutions and accumulate verified credentials. Future work should also focus on designing governance and trust frameworks that define participation policies, compliance requirements, and interoperability standards for entities operating within decentralized financial identity networks.

- **Data Management and Privacy**

  Future implementations may extend the proposed architecture to support dynamic and lightweight access policies and revocation mechanisms. While the proposed solution relies on CP-ABE to enforce static access policies, this approach may lead to performance challenges on resource-constrained devices when evaluating complex policy trees. Related to performance, Offloading parts of policy enforcement to edge nodes may improve scalability and reduce latency in decentralized environments. Lastly, incorporating zero-knowledge proofs could enable selective disclosure of credential attributes and privacy-preserving revocation is another important research direction.

- **Web 3.0 and NFTs**

  The intersection of SSI with Web 3.0 applications presents new opportunities for decentralized identity applications. Future work may extend the proposed wallet implementation into browser-based environments and integrate it directly with decentralized marketplaces. Related to Web 3.0, further research on identity bound tokens, and verifiable asset provenance are emerging research topics.

- **User Experience**

  User experience remains a critical factor in the success of decentralized identity systems. Although security research has increasingly recognized the importance of usability, relatively little work has addressed the challenges of managing cryptographic keys and consent mechanisms in user-facing applications (e.g., key loss and recovery, consent mechanism). Future work should investigate user-centered approaches to key management, recovery workflows, and consent management interfaces to ensure that SSI systems remain both secure and accessible to non-technical users.

- **Deployment, Governance, and Operational Models**

  The economic incentives and operational requirements associated with deploying and maintaining SSI infrastructures require further study. Future research should analyze the incentives for organizations to participate in decentralized identity networks and explore sustainable governance models that balance decentralization with operational efficiency.

  Equally important is the development of interoperable policies and standards for SSI participants. Many SSI ecosystems currently suffer from fragmentation across networks and protocols. Identity issuers, verifiers, and wallet providers must adhere to consistent specifications for credential generation, storage, validation, and exchange. Without clear governance frameworks and standardized protocols, fragmented interpretations of SSI specifications may hinder interoperability and trust. Recent developments also indicate that SSI principles are increasingly being adopted within regulated digital identity frameworks. Many emerging systems combine user-controlled wallets with institutional trust registries operated by governments or trusted organizations. Understanding how these hybrid identity architectures balance decentralization with regulatory oversight represents an important direction for future research.

  Another key research challenge involves determining the appropriate degree of decentralization in identity systems. Certain operations such as identity issuance, credential revocation, and secure storagemay still require partial centralization. Identifying the optimal balance between decentralization and operational practicality remains an important topic for future investigation.

  Finally, the scalability and performance of underlying blockchain infrastructures must be carefully evaluated. Many SSI architectures require frequent interactions with distributed ledger infrastructures, and a single identity transaction may involve multiple blockchain operations. Assessing the scalability, operational costs, and performance characteristics of these infrastructures will be essential to ensuring the long-term viability of decentralized identity systems.

Final Remarks

Identity remains a foundational pillar of trust in digital systems. As digital services continue to expand across financial, governmental, and social domains, the need for secure and privacy-respecting identity infrastructures becomes increasingly critical. Consequently, identity and access management remains a dynamic and multidisciplinary area within cybersecurity that requires sustained research, experimentation, and cross-sector collaboration.

Although Self-Sovereign Identity is not a universal solution and remains an evolving paradigm, the results presented in this dissertation demonstrate that carefully designed user-centric architectures can address many of the limitations associated with traditional identity management systems. By enabling individuals to control their digital identities and cryptographic assets while minimizing unnecessary data disclosure, SSI represents a meaningful step toward more transparent, privacy-preserving, and resilient digital identity ecosystems in an era increasingly shaped by data exploitation, large-scale data breaches, and surveillance capitalism.

Appendix A

Research and Industry Impact of the Dissertation

This dissertation has made sustained and measurable contributions to the fields of self-sovereign identity, decentralized key management, and privacy-preserving digital identity systems. Beyond advancing theoretical understanding, the research presented in this thesis has demonstrably influenced subsequent academic research, industrial innovation, and applied system design across multiple domains.

The impact of this work is reflected through citation metrics, reuse of proposed frameworks in real-world systems, references in patents, and recognition in systematic studies and bibliometric analyses. This appendix summarizes the academic, industrial, and societal impact of the dissertation and its associated publications.

A.1 Scholarly and Research Impact

The core publications associated with this dissertationincluding work on SSI architectures, decentralized client onboarding, practical key recovery, and access-controlled data sharinghave collectively received more than **410 academic citations** and over **8,000 reads on**

ResearchGate. These indicators reflect sustained interest from both the research community and industry practitioners.

A bibliometric study of scientific production on self-sovereign identity [310] reported that the authors of [190], [209], [109], and [311], namely R. Soltani, U. T. Nguyen, and A. An, rank among the **most influential contributors** in SSI research, based on citation-based metrics such as citation counts, h-index, and g-index. This recognition highlights the role of this body of work in shaping the research landscape of decentralized identity systems. The dissertations contributions have been cited extensively in:

- peer-reviewed journal articles and international conference proceedings [312], [313],
- doctoral dissertations and masters theses [314], [315],
- systematic literature reviews and mapping studies [316], [317],
- comparative and benchmarking evaluations of SSI frameworks [318], [319].

These citations indicate that the work is not merely referred to but actively used as a foundation for subsequent research, system design, and empirical evaluation.

Impact of "*A Survey of Self-Sovereign Identity Ecosystem*" [190]. An examination of the scholarly literature citing *A Survey of Self-Sovereign Identity Ecosystem* shows that this work has become a widely referenced foundation for research on decentralized identity systems. The survey is cited by **188 peer-reviewed publications**, including several highly influential works with more than **100 citations according to Google Scholar**, indicating its role as a key reference in the SSI research landscape.

Notably, the survey is cited by a highly referenced study on decentralized autonomous organizations and blockchain governance [320], which uses SSI concepts to motivate identity and trust mechanisms in decentralized organizational structures. It is also cited by a widely referenced analysis of blockchain transparency and organizational trust published in *Electronic Markets* [321], which applies SSI principles to enterprise adoption, compliance, and accountability. In addition, the survey informs a highly cited IEEE Access framework on blockchain-based identity management [322], where SSI is positioned as a core architectural component for digital identity verification and interoperability.

Across the citing literature, the survey is most frequently associated with use cases such as decentralized identity architectures, privacy-preserving authentication, governance and trust in blockchain systems, and large-scale enterprise and platform adoption. The repeated citation of this work by high-visibility surveys and applied frameworks demonstrates its influence in structuring how SSI ecosystems are defined, compared, and evaluated across multiple research domains.

A.2 Impact on Digital Client Onboarding and KYC Systems

One of the central applied contributions of this dissertation is the introduction of an SSI-based digital client onboarding framework built on distributed ledger technology (Hyperledger Indy). The framework addresses long-standing inefficiencies in traditional KYC processes by enabling identity reuse, minimizing data duplication, and preserving user privacy.

Subsequent research has described this framework as an *innovative framework* and an *in-*

novative client onboarding strategy, and it has served as the architectural basis for multiple later systems. More significantly, according to IEEE Xplore the framework has been cited in **20 international patents**, demonstrating direct industrial and commercial relevance [323, 324, 325].

The proposed onboarding model has been reused or extended in application domains including:

- financial services and decentralized KYC infrastructures [326], [327],
- event ticketing systems and secondary market control [328],
- land registry platforms and environmental sustainability systems [329],
- decentralized information systems and public-sector identity services [330].

This breadth of reuse illustrates the generality, practicality, and adaptability of the proposed framework beyond its original use case.

An analysis of the literature citing [209] further demonstrates that the onboarding model has influenced both applied and field-defining research in SSI. The paper is cited by several highly influential works with more than **100 citations each according to Google Scholar**, including comprehensive surveys and systematic mapping studies that shape research directions in decentralized identity. Notably, a widely referenced enterprise-focused survey on blockchain-based identity management [331] discusses deployment considerations such as regulatory compliance, trust models, and integration with existing enterprise systems. Across the citing literature, the work is most commonly associated with digital client onboarding, KYC processes, identity verification in regulated environments, and privacy-preserving credential exchange.

A.3 Impact on Decentralized Key Management and Wallet Security

Another major contribution of this dissertation is the development of a **practical decentralized key recovery protocol** for SSI-based digital wallets. Key management remains a critical barrier to SSI adoption, and the proposed protocol addresses this challenge by combining threshold cryptography with decentralized trust assumptions.

The proposed key recovery model has had significant downstream impact:

- it has been used as a **benchmark** in comparative evaluations of key recovery mechanisms [319],
- it has been recommended as a **state-of-the-art key management approach** in multiple applied systems [332].

The protocol has been referenced or adopted in applications addressing:

- secure access to electronic health records [333],
- agricultural and supply-chain management systems [334],
- resident-centric digital wallet experiences evaluated by public-sector organizations [335].

These applications demonstrate that the proposed model balances cryptographic rigor with usability and deployability.

A.4 Broader Societal and Policy Relevance

Globally, an estimated 850 million people lack formal identification, limiting access to healthcare, financial services, employment, and civic participation. Governments and international organizations are increasingly exploring digital identity solutions to address this gap.

By advancing privacy-preserving, user-centric identity architectures, this dissertation contributes technical foundations that support inclusive and trustworthy digital identity systems. The proposed models emphasize user control, decentralization, and compliance with privacy-by-design principles, making them particularly relevant in regulated and high-risk environments.

A.5 Summary of Key Impact Contributions

The impact of this dissertation can be summarized as follows:

- Introduced foundational SSI architectures that are widely cited and reused in academic research.
- Proposed an SSI-based digital onboarding framework cited by **over 20 patents** and real-world systems.
- Developed a practical decentralized key recovery protocol adopted as a benchmark and recommended solution.
- Influenced multiple application domains, including finance, healthcare, agriculture,

and public services.

- Achieved international recognition through bibliometric analyses of SSI research output.
- Contributed to positioning Canada among the leading contributors to SSI research.

A.6 Quantitative Impact Summary

Table A.1 summarizes the quantitative indicators of the dissertations academic and industrial impact.

Impact Metric	**Observed Value**
Total citations (core SSI papers)	>350
Total ResearchGate reads	>8,000
Patents citing the work	>20
Distinct application domains influenced	6
Theses/dissertations building on the work	Multiple
Bibliometric recognition in SSI research	Top contributors

Table A.1: Quantitative summary of the academic and industrial impact of the dissertation and its associated publications.

www.ingramcontent.com/pod-product-compliance
Lightning Source LLC
LaVergne TN
LVHW010719061126
851857LV00014B/1258
9781962116596